On Wings
and
Wheels

On Wings and Wheels

a dialogue on moral conflict. . .

SWAMI CHINMAYANANDA

Central Chinmaya Mission Trust
Bombay

© **Central Chinmaya Mission Trust**

First Edition		1991	-	5000 copies
Reprint		1995	-	5000 copies
Reprint	October	2004	-	1000 copies
Reprint	September	2006	-	1000 copies

Published by :
CENTRAL CHINMAYA MISSION TRUST
Sandeepany Sadhanalaya,
Saki Vihar Road, Mumbai - 400 072. India.
Tel.   : 091-22-2857 2367/ 5806 / 2828
Fax   : 091-22-2857 3065
Email   : ccmt@vsnl.com
Website : www.chinmayamission.com

Distribution Centre in USA:
CHINMAYA MISSION WEST
Publications Division
560 Bridgetown Pike,
Langhorne, PA 19053, USA
Tel.: (215) 396-0390 Fax:(215) 396-9710
www.chinmayapublications.org
publications@chinmaya.org

Printed by:
MAGIC PRINTS
233/234, Hindustan Kohinoor Ind.Complex,
L .B.S. Marg, Vikhroli (E), Mumbai - 400 083.
Tel.: 091-22-6796 9657/ 82 Tel.Fax: 091-22-6796 9657
Email: magicprints_graphics@yahoo.com

Price : Rs.70.00

ISBN : 81-7597-267-X

CONTENTS

Part Three
SPECIFIC ENQUIRIES ON SOCIAL ETHICS

Preface

The discussion that forms the context of this book has a curious background to it, the background of Wings and Wheels.

During a spiritual camp in 1984 at Sidhbari in the Himalayas, the idea of clarifying certain points on Ethics came up, with the intention of using the answers to make a souvenir booklet to be released during a talk series by H.H. Swami Chinmayananda in New Delhi. When this thought was presented to Swamiji he replied, "What! Where have I got the time? Can't you see there is not a minute to spare? If I started answering questions for every souvenir, I'd have no time to do any work!" Saying this he almost ended the matter. He then softened the blow a little by adding, "The only time I can spare is when I am in a car, a plane or a train — only in transition—that's the only time when I have no work to do. You can ask me your questions then!" Swamiji looked satisfied at having been so tactful in declining my request.

I was not disappointed. After all, the world's greatest message of the Bhagawad Gītā was delivered from a chariot with the added distraction of the din and roar of a battlefield.

The greatness of Indian holy men is that they never go back on their word! Even if they make what looks like a "mistake" they live through it until the effect is over.

Thus at the end of the camp I requested a back seat from the owner of the car in which Swamiji was to travel to Pathankote. Winding our way down the picturesque hilly road with its occasional ruins of the area and amidst Swamiji's comments on the scenic beauty of the Kangra Valley, emerged our very first discussion.

During that week I had been reflecting over the problem of Ethics and had formulated some questions in my mind but Swamiji completely confounded me in the very beginning by answering the first question in the reverse order to my expectation! When I asked "What is the criterion that makes an action good or bad," I expected him to say "motive" and my next questions were to have been on this subject. He flustered me when he answered "reaction". This broke the formality and resulted in our discussions becoming more of a conversation rather than a strict question and answer format.

I had intended to go home when we arrived in New Delhi but Swamiji was leaving for Kanpur immediately and after all, as long as we were on "Wheels" he could not back out of answering my queries. The session continued in the car between Kanpur and Lucknow. I was so eager to continue the session that I would have gladly followed him to Calcutta the following day but there was no seat on the plane!

The next opportunity came on "Wings" during the summer of 1985 in Europe and later on a flight from London to Washington. We were travelling at double the speed of sound, and amidst the noise we could make little headway.

Apart from my own questions two young ladies, Meera Bharany and Jyoti Chauhan teaching in New Delhi colleges, had also armed me with their questionaire. Wherever their names appear in the book, please note that the questions were theirs but asked by "proxy".

The next few interviews were on flights in U.S.A. and Canada including Philadelphia to Dayton and from Dayton to St. Louis. At St. Louis we had to change planes for Houston. While waiting in the airport lounge we sat facing the large windows. St. Louis is a T.W.A. terminal and eleven of their planes were lined up gracefully near the chute with their tails up in dignity and their wings spread out. It was during this very relaxed waiting period that Swamiji suggested that we call the book *On Wings and Wheels*.

I had followed Swamiji all around the world just because in a weak moment he promised to answer all my questions while travelling in the air or by car *On Wings and Wheels*. There are two morals to this story:

"Think twice before making a promise;"

"Persistance pays."

It was months afterwards that we discussed vegetarianism in Uttarkasi and a year later that I landed amidst a million coconut trees in Ernakulam, Kerala, Swamiji's birth place. During the car ride to the temple at Guruvayoor, Swamiji wrote what is written below in his handwriting. On the flight from Trivandrum he clarified certain points and then in Madras he put a complete stop and sent me home! I was flying back alone when I remembered his advice which, incidently, constitutes the third moral to this story:

"When an action becomes a habit it is time to wean oneself away by going in moderation!"

– Anjli Singh

Friends,
How do you get rid of such persistant pursuers whose intentions are so noble?

Upon Om, Atman, your Self,
place your meditation.
Glory unto you in your far–away
journey beyond darkness.

- Mundaka Upaniṣhad

On Wings . . .

. . . and Wheels

"Earth is round
Earth moves
Not seen but true
Sky is blue
Sunset is golden
Seen but false
Energy in the atom
Vitality in the sun
Gravitational force
Not Seen but true
Double moon
Mirage waters
Dream and hallucinations
Seen but false
World we see but not true
Truth we see not but true"

On Wheels ...

... Sometimes Off-Wheels.

*"No action is absolutely good
or absolutely bad.
Action itself is in a relative world,
it is not in the absolute.
Action is a relative
manifestation of reality."*

The Wheels started rolling and the Wings gliding at Sidhbari, situated against the challenging range of Dhauladhar, Himalayas.

*"In rational thinking, you are judging
the thing happening today
with reference to your entire past experience,
called wisdom,
which is recorded in the memory.
With reference to that
we try to judge the present.
The more you compromise with it,
the more the conscience is ill at ease."*

PART ONE

GENERAL ETHICS

What is Morality?

Anjli: Swamiji, how would you interpret the words ethics and morality?

Swamiji: The right and healthy values of life that you preserve in yourself comprise ethics, while morality is manifest in your behaviour vis-a-vis the outer world. Immoral thoughts are not possible. There are either unethical thoughts, or ethical thoughts. There is no ethical action, but moral and immoral activity. The two words are used in this sense: one is for the discipline of one's behaviour in the outer world and in one's relationships; the other is subjective—ethical values and moral behaviour. So unless you have got healthy ethical values you cannot live a healthy moral life.

Anjli: Would you say that ethics is the theoretical aspect?

Swamiji: No, the subjective. Ethics is more subjective, something you have to cultivate in yourself. Then its expression in the world outside becomes morality. A bad man ethically cannot be morally good. A moral man springs from the ethical values he preserves in himself.

Is Morality Inborn or Cultivated?

Meera: Is man naturally a moral being or is morality something that emerged because of the needs of the social situation?

Swamiji: It all depends on your definition of man. Man is an animal. He is a two-legged animal. A newborn baby has no sense of morality. Then we slowly train him, tame him, which in society we call giving him culture, education, etc. It is then that morality comes. Suppose you are living on a solitary island, morality would have no meaning then. Morality and self-discipline are necessary when you live in society.

Meera : In pre-historic times was there no morality?

Swamiji In pre-historic days there were caves, where there lived, not a single individual but his wife and children along with him, and the neighbours too.

Meera : Since man has always been a social animal, then morality has always existed?

Swamiji: Yes. But morality will depend upon the social complexion of the society. There was no income tax in the cave man's life. But sharing with the other man what he had, helping him in need lest he may also need him. It's mutual. I think morality slowly built up that way.

Meera: So, it is a give and take situation, and not inborn? But some religions insist morality is inborn.

Swamiji: No.

Meera: Do you mean to say it's only because, let's say, you may fall sick and need help from another later so you do it for him when he needs it, a kind of social contract?

Swamiji: Naturally. But that is the lowest level of human evolution. From the highest standpoint all individuals are nothing but the Supreme Reality, *Brahman*. So, you are only Me in that form. Me, meaning the Self, in that form. So, between you and Me, the relationship is like that between my hand and my leg.

Meera: Then at a higher standpoint morality comes naturally?

Swamiji: Yes, it comes naturally! It is not morality thrust upon from outside. In the beginning it is a discipline thrust upon from outside, later on it becomes natural for you to live those higher values.

Meera: Does the place of morality in the scheme of things come after birth?

Swamiji: Much afterwards. Because in the early childhood there is no morality. The child wants the other boy's toys without sharing his own. Then the mother and others tell him, "No, no, baby, you give it to that boy also. Play together." very slowly, we try to make him understand.

The Criterion of Judging an Action

Anjli: What is the criterion that makes an action right or wrong? How do we judge its moral worth?

Swamiji: Having performed an action, its reaction in the form of agitation, disturbance, self criticism, or an accusation shows that the action was wrong. And that action which in its perpetration brings peace, contentment, or self-congratulation to the mind is a good action. According to Hinduism, that which gives you sorrow do not give to others but do unto others as you would do to yourself. You know the saying, the same says the Bible. Therefore a morally good or morally bad act depends upon whether the action gives you regret or joy. In the case of the former it is a sin, or a morally bad action.

Psychological Reaction

Anjli: That means one's psychological reaction is the criterion?
Swamiji: Yes.
Anjli: What brings about this psychological reaction?
Swamiji: The past experience, that is called wisdom.
Anjli: But what about the first experience. With what wisdom does a man judge his action?
Swamiji: Yes, in the first experience the act is judged as instinct. In the beginning he just does it on the impulse of the moment, inspired by the moment. Remember he is an animal. Then he trains himself to become more and more tuned up as a member of the community or a member of a decent, cultured civilized society. Morality is not one law everywhere. There are some fundamentals which are common to all.
Anjli: Then according to this, morality will become a trial and error method?
Swamiji: No.
Anjli: But you would not know till after the event whether an action is good or bad. One should know before acting.
Swamiji: No, each one will have to learn it for himself through his own experiences. Any amount of thrusting from outside will not do.
Anjli: But there are hundreds of experiences you meet in life, that you face for the first time and to have deal with, without any prior wisdom.
Swamiji: Yes.
Anjli: Does that mean every time you have to first live through a situation in order to see whether you have made a mistake and to know how to handle it the next time?
Swamiji: But by that time, you get a third sense, a "sixth" sense as it were. So what will be my reaction if, suppose, I take this? You will know it. Just as you know how much you have to eat or drink. Every day you have to eat.
Anjli: Surely this must be with reference to something, with which you can presuppose or assume what your reaction will be? What is that?
Swamiji: Your own experience. For if a vegetarian unconsciously ate a little nonvegetarian food, he will have a reaction, a tremendous reaction. But a man who was a nonvegetarian and later became a vegetarian, a very strict vegetarian, no doubt, his reaction would be

different.

Anjli: What makes this reaction so different?

Swamiji: Mental composition. Your mental composition. There is no other way. The thing happening is outside. Who is reacting? The mind is reacting. The mind with its past is that which is reacting. I am a vegetarian, a strict vegetarian, what does that mean? My father was and my family was and I have thought over it and convinced myself, that vegetarianism is the best, so I am also a vegetarian. Then if I unconsciously eat some nonvegetarian food, my mind reacts to it very powerfully.

Anjli: One cannot say outright that an act is good or bad? What matters is how I react to it though my own experience?

Swamiji: Right you are! Right you are! In the final analysis it is so, but there are morally some instructions given because all of us are not on the same level of evolution. Moral rules are not common to all. That's why the *dharma** of a creative thinker is different from the *dharma* of a soldier. A thinker won't feel like even killing an insect. Why? Because he starts thinking, "Oh, I killed it, I should not have killed it". He reacts. A soldier could even kill a man. He may not have second thoughts because he is a soldier, his attitude is different.

Anjli: Are certain standards put forth by religion, others by society and also by the individual himself?

Swamiji: No, they all common.

Anjli: What is that common standard?

Swamiji: There are certain common standards which religion talks about and gives guidelines for. But each person will have to feel for himself what is right for him, what is going to be his particular specific reaction based on his past experience. Even in an ordinary conversation you ask yourself whether you should say such a thing or not. You know it from your own experience. There are some people with big mouths. They put their foot in their mouth. But cultured people, they pause for a moment, "Shall I say this? I may be joking but will it be understood as a joke?" All in a split moment you calculate and decide and only then you say it. Especially professional speakers. There is no time for them to think because one sentence follows another. But as you go on practising, it becomes very easy for you to discriminate one thing from the other. Just as in the world the grain merchants will be able to grade a grain just by looking at it, just by touching it. In the same way jewellers can tell which is a true diamond, which is a second rate or third rate one. In the same way, when you are sensitive enough, giving

---

* The right way of living depending upon one's psychological nature.

minimum unhappiness to others, whatever you do will be morally good.

Anjli: So the criterion of a morally good action is whether or not it brings to one's mind happiness and tranquility?

Swamiji: Well all right! A sense of peace, a sense of fulfilment, a sense of joy are signs of morally good actions. Whereas an action that brings back to the mind "Why did I do it? I should not have done it" will be immoral for you, although to another individual it may be a moral thing because he does not react in the same way. Morality is not standardized. Except in only a few matters. What do you call them?.... The commandments! Disciplines given to and common to everybody. Adultery, stealing and things like these are common to all. Everybody will feel it. If not immediately, then later, you think "I should not have done it". By following commandments laid down by religion and living a disciplined life makes the mind calm and peaceful.

Anjli: To make tranquillity and peace of mind as a standard of judgment is very tricky. You can achieve this peace of mind even through drugs.

Swamiji: We are talking of the calmness that is the result of right action and not of drugs!

Anjli: Well, I mean that because of the action of taking drugs I got peace of mind, then the act of taking drugs becomes morally right, if "peace of mind" is the criterion.

Swamiji: Yes!

Anjli: I mean, I am speaking from a theoretical point.

Swamiji: No, you are not. From the theoretical point also it is wrong. Because the man who is taking drugs knows what he is taking but he is helpless.

Anjli: Oh! Oh! You are saying he knows he is doing something wrong but earlier, Swamiji, you said he comes to learn only after the experience.

Swamiji: It is because of the past experience that he has gained the knowledge.

Anjli: That means first time he took the drugs.....

Swamiji: You cannot blame him. The first time a man takes drinks he does not know it is bad. Then in his reaction he finds that, "No, my father was unhappy or he will be unhappy if he comes to know of it." Then, he does it secretly. Why? Because now he knows that a sense of guilt is always there, otherwise he would have done it openly. And if he continues drinking, it could become a habit and later on he might become an alchoholic and then he would be helpless.

Anjli: Which means that so long as a person does not get into the habit, for him that action is right. If he does not become a drug addict, for him to take drugs once in a while is all right? Well, with drugs you can't say that because, it is far more quickly habit-forming. Let's take drinks. A person who has a little weakness for drinks, who takes one or two drinks a day just for enjoyment?

Swamiji: Nothing wrong in it.

Anjli: Nothing wrong?

Swamiji: What is wrong in it? Drinking by itself is morally neither good nor bad. It may be bad for health. Some doctors would say it is bad or there may be some doctors who might recommend it and prescribe it. See, everything in moderation. Where you drink it's alright but let not the drink drink you.

Anjli: Wait a minute!

Swamiji: "Moderation" only because it was you who in the first place said that if there are certain weaknesses in you, how do you come out of them? At such times don't try to stop but go in moderation and slowly wean yourself out from the negative tendencies. It is only in that sense that "moderation" was said.

Anjli: That means only if you have a weakness would moderation follow.

Swamiji: Naturally! Everybody has got some weakness.

Anjli: But you would not recommend moderation if you have not started it. I mean you would not say it is all right to drink once in a while if you have not got a weakness for it.

Swamiji: Why should I? But incase you are already entangled by a weakness, a slave to a habit, then the best way is to do it in moderation and then try to get out of it.

Anjli: Sometimes our inner impulses get the better of our understanding. Smoking, for instance.

Swamiji: A weakness is always a weakness and no seeker has a right to perpetuate it; no institution should entertain the audacity to argue for it, because it can drag you down.

Anjli: Let's take the example of sex. If it does not have a reaction on you, is it all right to go ahead and have fun?

Swamiji: It's all right, really speaking. But if there is no reaction then why should you go through those convulsions?

Anjli: "No reaction" in the sense of guilt, that "I should not have done it" but, if on the contrary someone feels "Yes, I'm glad I did it". then?

Swamiji: Then, in that case there is nothing wrong. That is why we prescribe *grahastha āshram*, marriage.

Anjli: That's all right. But what about sex outside marriage? Supposing it does not have an adverse reaction, would one be justified?

Swamiji: I think it will have a reaction and it could bring back to you disastrous consequences. Rāvana was a mighty power, but because of his inordinate desires, his mental vitality was retarded and inwardly he collapsed. I am not talking about the external collapse when he was vanquished. That's not it. Mentally his peace was gone, his judgment was gone and he came to a point of even wanting to destroy the messenger of Rāma. This was wrong. Although in his own way he was a great man, he should have respected ambassadors. He had lost his mental equipoise in the upsurge of passionate desire for another man's wife. So it was morally wrong.

Anjli: Rāvana was disturbed because he did not get what he wanted. Now supposing a person does get what he wants, then why should it disturb him if he does not have any moral compunction?

Swamiji: You are contradicting yourself. Yes, we are asking of the moral values about it. If he has no moral compunction, he is only an animal. A seed bull.

Anjli: What I mean is that when your conscience has no complaint about an action and also you get what you desired and it does not retard your mental vitality in frustraion, then is it wrong if you indulge in it?

Swamiji: It depends upon the individual. Suppose the individual is not sensitive to any such thing. He is only a seed-bull.

Motive

Anjli: Don't motives count in the ethical worth of an action?

Swamiji: Yes. For example, a surgeon uses a knife in the operation theatre to save a patient's life, and even though the patient may die it cannot be called a sin, whereas the act of killing somebody with the same knife for personal gain is decidedly sinful. The merit depends upon the motive of the act.

Anjli: If an action is to be judged good or bad by its motive, which of the several complex motives involved in any one action are to be taken as the main standard of judgment?

Swamiji: There can be only one motive; its branches will be the other motives. There is only one motive.

Anjli: But when I give charity I can have several motives in giving away the money.

Swamiji: Then it is not charity.

Anjli: No?

Swamiji: Giving money or signing a cheque is not charity.

Anjli: Let's say the act of giving money, may have several motives.

Swamiji: Yes, according to the motive, it will be charity or something else.

Anjli: I may feel kindness toward somebody and give him some money. But at the same time I know that people are watching me, and at the back of my mind I feel I will get some applause. On the other hand, I may be getting some income-tax relief, or maybe I want to balance out some guilt about having cheated someone earlier, or something. So there are several motives involved in giving away the money.

Swamiji: Then it will be the cumulative or the average of all these motives that will decide the result of it. That's why the *Karma Phala Data** is *Iśvara*, the Lord. So many factors go into the determination of the final result of an action. Even a computer may not be able to sort it out. That is why the Lord is called the Supreme Intelligence. So when you do an action and then surrender it to Him, He judges the moral worth of the action, and the results come back to you in the form of what you meet in life.

Anjli: Should the totality of motives be taken into account?

Swamiji: The totality of motives must play into it, but then for your practical purposes you should only think in terms of how far am I? By giving this am I trying to gain joy and a sense of fulfilment and satisfaction or is it going to disturb me? Suppose your main motive was only the applause which you did not get, your action will bring you only disappointment. Then it is not a morally good one. It is not charity. You with that amount are showing off and in this way you are trying to purchase something to further your vanity.

Anjli: That means the result of your action is directly related to the totality of motive, the motive with which you give.

Swamiji: Yes, naturally! That is why I said every action, even in secular law is calculated by means of the motive behind it.

Anjli: An action may be prompted by dual or complex motives which may be mixed in being both lofty and base at the same time, for example, money given out of kindness as well as for recognition. If the action is to be judged not by one motive but by the totality of motives, then no action is absolutely good or absolutely bad, it can only be predominantly good or predominantly bad.

Swamiji: Yes, that is true. Really speaking, an action itself is neither good nor bad. And you cannot say it is absolutely bad or absolutely good. It is relative. Action itself is in the relative world. It is not in the absolute.

Anjli: Krishna also says in the Bhagavad Gītā that all actions are riddled with imperfection. Is it a fact that there can be no absolutely good

* The dispenser of the fruits of action.

action?

Swamiji: Action itself is a relative manifestation of reality, a delusion. So in that action how can there be an absolutely good action?

Means

Anjli: When the means are bad, yet the motive is good, what is the action? Good or bad?

Swamiji: Bad means could never bring about a good result even if the motive were great. Because by mixing potassium cyanide and hydrochloric acid one cannot get a nice edible chutney.

Anjli: You have been saying motive is the criterion and now suddenly you say means have to be good and that motive does not come into account. Won't that falsify everything you said earlier? Let us be very logical. If the means are "bad" but the motive is "good" and you say this action is to be termed "bad", then the earlier contention that motive is the determining factor is falsified. If, on the other hand, you say such an action is to be termed "good" then man would get freedom to employ all kinds of means and society would become rampant with Robin Hoods. One would justify even use of drastic means to control population in over-populated countries and fanatics converting by force.

Swamiji: Ha! Ha! Ha! No! That is not logical at all. When the motive is good, the means will be good and the end will be great. And even if the end is calamitous you have done no wrong because your motive was good. When the motive is chaste nobody will go by immoral methods to reach the conceived goal. It is logical that cause determines the effect. The means means what? Means is not something outside you.

Anjli: So, actually the motive and the means are related.

Swamiji: Naturally, because the motive, the values that you uphold in life determine the quality of the thoughts; the quality of thoughts determine in turn the quality of actions. Let us say that to pass an exam is your motive. So you prepare all the questions and answers and replace them in the examination hall. Ugh! You may pass, but in the long run your crime may be detected, and in any case, you will always live with the guilt.

Anjli: Robin Hood gave away all that he stole to the poor. But the means were bad. He stole in order to give.

Swamiji: That's why Robin Hood was caught in the end.

Anjli: Yes, but, as far as his action was concerned people praise Robin Hood and they recount his adventures as examples of generosity.

Swamiji: The idea is stupid. People can be made to praise. You give them plenty. People will praise. A dictator is sometimes popular even if he allows corruption to run uncontrolled. Such a one might become unpopular if he tried to stop corruption.

Anjli: That means Robon Hood's motive wasn't good.

Swamiji: What was his motive? Not to "distribute," but to "loot and distribute." That is not a good motive. He did not help the poor people work hard to enable them to come out of their poverty. There was nothing creative in Robin Hood's motive. Bandits would be considered good then.

Anjli: Man's motives sometimes appear excellent but we feel bound to condemn the consequential action. For instance, in the case of a fanatic converter we would have to say that his motive is not only to just convert but to forcefully convert or to bribe and convert. He should rather try to convince a person on rational or humane grounds or provide a superior and beneficial model worthy of emulation. Then alone would conversion to an idea have value.

Swamiji: Good thought! But again you are thinking in terms of others' judgment of the fanatic. Moral judgment here refers to others judging another's morality.

Anjli: Then let's take one's own judgment of oneself.

Swamiji: Yes, yes. If you are a fanatic, for example, you must be forgiven because you don't see your mistake, until a time comes when you suddenly feel that, "Oh, I wasted twenty years in fanatic misconception."

Anjli: Great crimes are committed in the name of religion sometimes.

Swamiji: Yes. Similarly, fanaticism can develop in politics also.

Happiness as the Standard

Anjli: "Maximum happiness for maximum number for maximum time" is Swamiji's motto. In making happiness a standard or criterion in action, would Swamiji consider more valuable, happiness that is intense, though short-lived or lesser happiness but extended to a longer time? Which is more valuable — *intensity* or *duration*?

Swamiji: The duration is more important at the social level. A scheme of life by which for a longer period of time a problem is solved and society can be reasonably happy.

Anjli: Happiness in *heaven* or happiness on *earth* (both are temporary according to the Vedas!)? I am asking a hypothetical question just in case heaven exists!

Swamiji: Here we will choose happiness in heaven because it is more intense, we are told. There the contact is a subtle body* with subtle objects. Therefore the intensity of happiness should be greater. That is why perhaps the *rishis*** have encouraged renouncing the sensual · pleasures here, in order to get the subtler joys for a longer period of time in the heavens. So in the context of your question, heavenly life should be better because it is more intense plus is longer in duration.

Anjli: Which is more valuable — *present* or *future* happiness in this life — and why? Which should be given precedence?

Swamiji: The present is the womb of the future. A greater future happiness can be had only by investing the present correctly. Look after the present and the future will look after itself.

Anjli: Can you clarify the difference between the types of happiness?

Swamiji: Happiness that arises from constant effort and inner self-control can yield a greater beauty and a larger sense of fulfilment. In the beginning its practice may be painful and arduous, but a person who has the necessary courage and heroism, to walk the precipitous path of self-purification, creativity, and inward balance comes to enjoy the subtlest happiness and the all-fulfilling sense of inner peace. The flimsy happiness that is gained through sense indulgence and sense gratification is a joy that is fleeting, vanishing as quickly as it comes, and after its onslaught there is a terrific undercurrent that upsets our equilibrium and drags us into ill-reputed dissipation. This happiness lasts only so long as the sense organs are actually in contact with sense objects.

Anjli: Why then are most of us tempted by this fleeting happiness? ·

Swamiji: Because its results are immediate. There is no waiting period and not much effort required.

Anjli: From where does happiness arise?

Swamiji: There is no intrinsic happiness in objects. The same objects do not please everybody. We associate happiness with the objects we desire. Happiness is the nature of the real Self of man which expresses and functions through his body, mind and intellect. This Self, expressing through a mind agitated with desires, throws shades of sorrow. The Self expressing through a mind unagitated, because of

* Subtle body means the mind-intellect equipment, the psychological personality, which is supposed to leave the body at the time of death. This equipment along with the *vasanas*, the innate tendencies, gathered by the individual through his interaction with the world, moves from one plane of experience to various other planes of experience without the help of the physical body according to its quality of thoughts and habits.
** Sages

desires satisfied or stilled, throws its own light of joy. Happiness lies within one's Self, as the Self and not in the objects outside.

Anjli: Which is more important — happiness of *another* or happiness of *oneself?*

Swamiji: Certainly of another. This is the crux of any religion. Aiming at happiness for oneself is selfish. Every animal does that.

Anjli: In choosing between happiness of another and happiness of myself, why should I give precedence to the other? I am speaking of the pursuit of happiness as akin to the pursuit of individual perfection.

Swamiji: If the word "happiness" is used in that sense of the term, your happiness comes first, because you are realizing the Self, the very source, the goal.

Anjli: If I use the word happiness in the other sense, still, why must I aim at another's happiness and not my own? The Upaniṣads state that man *does* act only for his own happiness so then what is the significance of saying he *ought* to seek another's happiness? A mother denying herself for the sake of the child is really doing so for her own happiness, for it would give her more pleasure to see her child happy. It would seem it is not possible to act only for the happiness of another!

Swamiji: You know the real happiness that man seeks is for himself, but the word "self" of "himself" is misunderstood as "I" the physical, the mental, the intellectual entity. So to avoid or end that *jīvatva bhāvanā* the feeling of limitation, that I am only the body, mind and intellect, we liquidate ourselves by taking interest in others. My actions are motivated not for my happiness, but for giving happiness to others. By thus working with the *Karma Yoga** spirit, the ego gets sublimated at which stage your state of mental poise takes you ultimately to your own satisfaction. When the ego is eliminated or sublimated or your viewpoint is uplifted, in the service of giving happiness to others, extraordinary changes take place within.... The mind within becomes quieter, a contemplative mood arises, and you ultimately come to experience absolute happiness. So there is no contradiction. The contradiction is only because of the misunderstanding of the word "self," from which we are calling upon you to wake up. Therefore it only appears there is a contradiction. Actually there is none.

Conflicting Standpoints

Anjli: In the 2nd chapter of the Bhagawad Gītā Krishna explains that it

---

* Offering one's actions to a higher goal.

was morally correct for Arjuna at that time to fight the battle. He considered the action from various standpoints and gave arguments in support of this. He first started from the highest philosophical standpoint (stanzas 11 to 25) then from the standpoint of glimmering consciousness in stanza 26. He further explains the materialistic standpoint in stanza 28, the sociological view in stanza 31, the standpoint of result (heaven) in stanza 32, of one's duty and station in life in stanza 33, and lastly from the standpoint of society's opinion. The question is, what if these standpoints happened to conflict? Supposing it were correct from one point and not from the other, should one still undertake the action? To which standpoint would one give precedence and how would one judge the greater value of one over the other?

Swamiji: The rule is simple: Sacrifice the individual benefit and take the larger interest into consideration. Personal sacrifice for the sake of the majority is the principle of ethics. Selfishness is unethical. The spring of unethical activity is selfishness. So in the case of conflict, always choose that which is beneficial to the largest number. If the contradiction is between you, your personal interest and the others, follow the example of Śri Rāmachandraji. His father would have been happy had he remained in Ayōdhya. The vast population would have been happy too. But in the long run interest of humanity, history would have recorded that, and we would have done likewise. The entire society would have suffered as a result. Therefore, for the sake of the entire world, *lōkasangrah*, Rāma maintained the idea of *dharma**. The standpoint of the world is greater than one's community. Your community is greater than your caste, your caste is greater than your family, your family is greater than you, yourself.

Moral Sensitivity

Anjli: Earlier in our discussion you had mentioned moral sensitivity. What has to be present in an individual to make him morally sensitive?

Swamiji: To make him sensitive you will have to train him. He must become more *sāttvic*.

Anjli: Please explain *sāttvic*.

Swamiji: The three *gunas*, *sattva*, *rajas* and *tamas*—are the three attitudes with which the mind functions. The psychological being in everyone comes under the influence of the three different "climatic conditions"

---

* Way of right living

of the mind and intellect. *Sattva* is perfect purity and luminosity. Under the *sattva* influence the mind is steady, reflecting ever faithfully the consciousness, the Self. Under the influence of *sattva* the mind is in an inspiring and creative mood, it is actually intelligent and capable of taking the longest flights into the realms of wisdom. On all such occasions of vast knowing and deep understanding and right choice, the inner equipment is under the influence of *sattva*.

Anjli: And *rajas?*

Swamiji: Where there is an onslaught of *rajoguna* in the bosom, man's mind is wrecked with a hundred painful passions, consisting of desires for things he has not yet acquired and an attachment to things that he possesses. Under the influence of *rajas* a man must necessarily and endlessly earn, spend, save, procure, procreate, protect, and yet thirst for more, be anxious for more, and be afraid to lose. He is whipped from action to action. Rushing through all his inexhaustible actions he is expressing the idea "I am the doer." He acts from an ego-centric point of view.

Anjli: How does a man act under *tamas?*

Swamiji: *Tamas* is born of ignorance. Under the influence of *tamas* man's intellectual capacity to discriminate between right and wrong gets veiled and he starts acting as if under some hallucination or stupefaction. Such a man lives in indolence, heedless of higher purposes, and asleep to the nobler and divine aspirations of life. There is no consistency of purpose, brilliance of thought, tenderness of emotion, or nobility of action in an individual who comes under the contamination of the *tamoguna* influences.

Anjli: Are all three present in an individual?

Swamiji: Yes, to varying degrees. The more often and more completely we go beyond *rajas* and *tamas* and make our bosom full of *sattva,* the more grows our capacity to observe, to analyze, to understand, and to become aware of the world outside and judge it correctly.

Anjli: Would it be *sattva* that would have to be present to make an individual morally sensitive?

Swamiji: Yes, if he is *tāmasic* and *rājasic* he will not feel the result of his actions. The looter, the plunderer, or the murderer doesn't feel. But when one becomes, sensitive, i.e. more *sāttvic,* then one becomes more and more sensitive to such things, to disharmony in society, in the world. It is something like music. Pop music cannot be experienced and enjoyed by one who is sensitive to classical music. And classical music cannot be enjoyed by one who wants rock 'n roll. Take language! One who is sensitive enough reads a book, but another throws it away.

Ah! style is necessary, he says.

Anjli: You say he has to be trained, and that it is through experience that morality comes?

Swamiji: Yes, at a given moment you take that which is morally good for you. It depends upon the grossness or the sensitivity of your mind, upon the *sattva* that you have cultivated. That is why the *dharma* of a *sudra* is different from the *dharma* of a *brahmin**. At each level the Scriptures have tried to prescribe that which is right and which is not. To a *sudra* drinking and nonvegetarianism is all right, even polygamy because the *sudra* is not sensitive. But for a *brahmin*, these actions are forbidden. Occasionally *ksatriyas* are allowed at the warfront some such things. Thus, each level has its own morality. As a *sannyasi*** you have to do certain things. That's your *dharma*. But you cannot prescribe the same to everybody.

My Station and its Duties

Anjli: Depending on one's evolutionary stage, would it be more advisable to follow a standpoint of lesser values as advised in the Bhagwad Gita, "Do one's duty according to the station in life." Any comment?

Swamiji: Yes. The *varnas** and *asramas**** are psychological evaluations. For whatever you are fit, depending on your temperament, and your constitution, likewise will be your duties. By following one's station in life one can serve the society more without inner conflicts. One may have *rajoguna* but he has *tamas* too, therefore he is a *vaisya*. As a *vaisya* he does agriculture and trade. There he will gain more mental peace and a sense of fulfilment than if he were to be in a *ksatriya's* state or doing a *brahmin's dharma*. So these *varnas* and *asramas* are very careful

---

* The four castes : Certain well-defined characteristics determine the four types of human beings; they are not always determined by heredity or accident of birth, though it has come to be misunderstood as such. The four fold classification is universal and for all times. In modern language the 1. *brahmin* 2. *ksyatriya* 3. *vaisya* 4. *sudra* may be called 1) the creative thinkers 2) leaders of men 3) the commercial employers 4) the labourers (the proletarians). Different types of duties are assigned to each of these classes depending upon their nature, which is ordered by the proportion of the *gunas* in the make-up of each type of mental temperament. By observing a person — his type of actions, the quality of his ego, the wisdom of his knowledge, the texture of his understanding, the temper of his fortitude, and the brilliance of his happiness, one can determine his caste and not by birth.

** rununciate

*** The four stages in life.

psychological classifications. The way of life or what should be one's way of life is all prescribed according to the psychological texture of the individual. So, your question depending upon evolutionary stages, yes! Depending upon the evolution of the mind is the *varṇa*, caste, category and in the *varṇa* also there are the stages, *āsramas*: *brahmacharya, grhastha, vanaprastha sannyasa**.

Anjli: Supposing there is a choice involved. Should you choose according to your station in life or should you choose keeping in mind the larger viewpoint? Supposing there was a conflict?

Swamiji: Choose from one's station in life. The war may be coming, but the *brāhmin* who takes up the gun will confuse matters. Let him stay where he is stationed in life and proceed according to the *karma*, work, that is allotted to him, the duties enjoined on him, according to his qualification, according to his psychological nature, his *dharma*. Doing his *dharma* he will be supporting or helping the war efforts.

Anjli: Even if the choice is between the highest goal and one's *dharma*?

Swamiji: All this is because you are identifying the issue with a particular problem. What if an engineer got worried because plague had spread. Suppose the engineer runs away from the area of his duty and enters into the plague area to serve the society, "So many are dying, you know, I must go there and work." He will be bringing chaos. Let the doctors all rush in there, not the engineers! So, from the highest standpoint, the Pure Self, your duty is to serve the society around you. Society is macrocosmic and not microcosmic. You must rise higher above your personal relationship centres to serve society. Take the example of the judge in England. His own son was on trial. The judge punished him with either life imprisonment or death and then got out of his chair, removed the black coat, and rushed and embraced his son. As a judge, he was not the father of anybody. It is another matter that the Queen pardoned the child. But where the judge was sitting, he did not behave like a father. That is why justice is blind. No such relationship can exist otherwise your discriminative power cannot play. Similarly as the commander-in-chief of the Pāndava forces, Arjuna is an army man. He has not to look into the enemy lines to see who is standing there. In the opposite line, too, they had no such consideration. Their *guru* Droṇacārya did not say, "After all they are my children, therefore, I won't fight against them."

---

* The four stages in life :
  i. student
  ii. house holder
  iii. retired person
  iv. renunciate

The Goal

Anjli: Is one *dharma* better than the other?

Swamiji: No, at a given level each one is right. By being loyal to our own level of feelings and ideas, to our development of consciousness, we can evolve into higher states of self-unfoldment.

Anjli: Which level is higher?

Swamiji: The highest level is wherein you are nearer to the $\bar{A}$tman, the Self, the concept that the whole universe is me, myself. To recognise yourself with the One, with the whole universe, feeling that I will not bring even a little harm to anyone, and I am in harmony with the entire universe is the highest state. Living then becomes effortless and creative. When one goes beyond the action-reaction stage, beyond good and evil and cause and effect then life becomes a recreation and a means of expressing the inner joy.

Anjli: From the level of the *vaiśya can* you reach the Supreme Self directly or will you have to go up by stages?

Swamiji: Without *sattva* you can never reach the Supreme. The rest is only various degrees of *rajas* and *tamas*.

Anjli: Would you have to go sequentially through the stages *śudra, vaiśya, kṣatriya,* and *brāhmin dharmas* to reach the Supreme Self, the reality?

Swamiji: Wherever you are, in whatever station, from there you have to reach *sattva* in varying degrees because *tamas* will be reduced only when the mind's agitations, *vikśepa,* are quietened. As agitations quieten, *sattva* increases slowly.

Anjli: So, ethics is evolutionary? One has to work towards creating *sattva* in order to reach the ultimate goal of finding one's Self.

Swamiji: Yes.

Anjli: Conclusively, it is to the standpoint of one's *dharma*, in whatever evolutionary stage one is, to which percedence, should be given, maintaining that the final goal is to reach a state beyond good and evil.

Swamiji: Yes!

Some Fallacies Counteracted

Regress ad infinitum

Anjli: If the goodness of an action is to be judged by the goodness of the motive, how would you judge the goodness of the motive? This could lead to *regress ad infinitum.*

Swamiji: No, all goodness is measured in terms of our identification with the Absolute. With reference to the Supreme alone we say an act is good or bad. You can put Righteousness or Goodness in place of the concept of God. He is the Absolute Good. It is with reference to Him that we say something is good or bad. That's why the Absolute Good, Absolute Kindness, Absolute Mercy, Absolute Power, these are the concepts of God. Why should we have a God? Without Him, moral values are not possible. What is the standard of comparison by which we can judge anything? The standard is — God, the Absolute. So there is no question of *regress ad infinitum!*

Double Criteria Ethics

Anjli: If an action is good or bad depending on the result or reaction received by the mind after the act, as well as on the *motive* prior to it, it becomes a *double criteria ethics* taking both motive as well as *psychological reaction* of the mind as standards of judgment. How would Swamiji reconcile the two statements?

Swamiji: The two are interconnected. Together they are called the values that a person upholds. As I said in the beginning the values with which you are thinking motivate your actions in the world outside. If the motive is pure, the action will be good, so let's always keep the mind as pure as possible. "Motive may be pure" means eliminate your ego, your selfishness. When, as I told you, the motive is for the benefit of others, *paropakarartham idam sariram*, it is pure. If the motive is pure, the action will be good. Having done the act if you have a moral doubt, "Did I do it rightly or wrongly?" or "How am I to judge?" the answer is: "By the result." I don't mean the outside result of the action, rather it is the result in yourself. The subjective result. Your reaction. The result outside may be a success. Thereby don't say that "I have done it rightly." That is not it. When the action springs forth from you, start looking to see if there is any selfishness and if it is really motivated by sheer love. "Hey! Stop!" If after having done the act there is mental perturbation and you have again got a feeling of doubt, "Did I do the right thing?" then understand that even though you thought that you did it selflessly, you had really compromised. The mind can hoodwink you into thinking you have surrendered, but you may not have. Therefore there is no contradiction between the two standards.

Time Fallacy

Anjli: Even if the two criteria, that is, motive and psychological result, are interconnected, still, if result is to be taken into account there would arise a *time fallacy*. One would never really know *before* the action whether it was good or bad till the psychological result sets in *after* the action.

Swamiji: No, why shouldn't one? That is what I told you earlier that you can train yourself to develop a "sixth" sense and come to know how you would react. That is why it is also said that you should renounce your anxiety for the fruits, the results thereof. Fruit can be in the future only. When the challenge came, you were discriminating and deciding how to react. And at the point where the reaction comes, those who had eliminated the ego will react beautifully. The grey areas are those where you are not sure what to do. There you take the help of the Lord, surrender to Him, and do what comes in the mind. Because it is a grey area. "Well, it can be this way or that way, both could be right."

Rāmachandraji's renunciation of Sitā, was it right or wrong? One way it is right, another way it is wrong. Then has he been ethically good? Yes, because he renounced his personal happiness for the sake of the public, and therefore ethically he is right.

The Moral Connoisseur

Anjli: At this point I would like to change the discussion from the topic of the reference point of action to the subjective aspect, that is, the instrument by which we judge an action to be right or wrong. Regarding the power in man that judges actions, is it an inexplicable faculty within ourselves by which laws are laid down? A kind of intuition? Is it intuition that judges? What is it in man that judges?

Swamiji: No, you cannot call it intuition because it is with the help of what he knows that one judges the situation. You could also call it intuition, but it is more the discriminating power within the intellect's faculties. For one who can *pause the mind more*, his judgment or discriminating power is more. Although the brain or the instrument may be the same, the clarity of vision and judgment of one who is disturbed can go beserk. But when the mind is relatively calm his judgment will not be so bad. Therefore, in that sense we can say judgment is intuitive.

Conscience

Anjli: A man's conscience may be the "conscience of an ass" (Ruskin) or a man may act conscientiously but in accordance with some defective standard, for example, a fanatic. Can you throw some light on this, especially as in these cases there is no angle of deviation from what one knows to be right and what one does and conscience would then be an inexplicable faculty.

Swamiji: Inexplicable? Conscience is with reference to what you already know. When I know a thing is wrong and then I do it, there is a contradiction between what I know and that I do. That is called conscience.

Anjli: If there is a certain rational judgment being formed in the mind then one should say it is a kind of a rational faculty that is working within and not a kind of an intuitive conscience.

Swamiji: In rational thinking you are only judging the thing that is happening today with reference to your entire past experience, called wisdom, which is recorded in the memory. With reference to that we try to judge the present. And the more you compromise with it the more the conscience is ill at ease.

Anjli: Conscience is nothing but the intellect then?

Swamiji: It's total memory. But it is not memory only. Memory is accumulated knowledge. The conscience is not intellect alone.

Anjli: This intellect judges according to the wisdom that it acquires.

Swamiji: Yes, exactly. Your own action. Not somebody's action.

The Conditioned Intellect

Anjli: The intellect judges not only with the help of wisdom acquired but also as you said earlier, *sattva*, *rajas*, and *tamas* envelop the intellect at the time of judgment.

Swamiji: Yes, it is the intellect that judges and the intellect's judgment would change according to the moods — *sattva*, *rajas*, *tamas*.

Anjli: So, conscience is intellect with its accumulated wisdom conditioned by the moods.

Swamiji: Yes, sure. And that's how the mistakes are made.

Anjli: Can we say the power that judges an action is the intellect conditioned by its moods and drawing on past experiences — all this together we could call conscience?

Swamiji: The intellect does include the experience of the past. Suppose all your experiences were forgotten—all the past. Say you are under drugs! There is no intellect, meaning no past experience memorized. Now you judge the present. The present is understood, evaluated by the mood of the mind. If the mind is slightly disturbed, your judgment and your interpretation of the data will be confused. Then you act. At the moment you acted as the intellect judged; later you realized that it was a mistake. That is why we say that a sin is only wrong judgment. But the judgment became wrong because of the mood of the mind. Had I been at that time quieter I would not have made that mistake.

The Ideal Judgment

Anjli: Can we say, the ideal action is that which is judged by the intellect together with its past experience in the mood of *sattva* and only here conscience could be called intuition?

Swamiji: *Sattva* means being able to quieten the agitations. That's why I said the person who can *pause the mind more*, whose judgment is without prejudice or favour, as in the case of Jesus, is correct. When the judgment is serene and calm you won't make any mistake.

Look at the judgment of Jesus when Mary Magdalene was brought on serious charges. According to the Old Testament, she should be stoned to death. Jesus did not revolt against the rule. Yes, it should be done, that is what is said in the Scriptures. You must do it. But who has the birthright to do so? Only the individual who had never sinned could throw the first stone. And Jesus walked away. What a precise, beautiful, discriminative judgment. Nobody dared touch a stone.

Anjli: Quite right. He did not say, "Don't punish."

Swamiji: No, but who were to punish? Had they the right to punish? Yes, provided they had never done anything wrong. The woman walked behind the Lord and became his great follower. So, you can say, right judgment is intuitional because Jesus had neither prejudice against nor in favour of that woman or the act. Therefore the judgment turned out to be perfect.

Reason and Goodness

Anjli: If that which is pure good is also that which is pure reason,
then will the completely rational man be the absolutely good one?
"The spiritual qualification of a philosopher is a condition for his
philosophizing properly". I read this in a book on ethics.

Swāmiji: It all depends on the quality of the reasoning. If one is *sāttvic*
then his reasoning will be good. If he is *rājasic* or *tāmasic*, he may be
rational, no doubt. Rāvana was rational. But the quality in him was
predominantly *rājasic*. Therefore, he rationalized everything that is
immoral. Duryodhana also did the same. " I know what is right but I
have not an inclination to do it. I know what is wrong but I cannot keep
away from it. I act impelled by some power lodged in my heart; as he
directs so I act"*.

Both men were highly intelligent, they had their own rational
arguments. So he has his own rational conclusion as to why he is
there. But the quality of his performance depended upon the
quality of the reason he had. Your statement is true if the condition
of the intellect is purely *sāttvic*.

Guidelines for Judgment

Anjli: Would Swamiji advise a *rājasic* or *tāmasic* man to be guided by
the moral judgment of a *sāttvic* person or should the person
evaluate his actions according to his own judgment, even though
imperfect?

Swāmiji: Yes, that is what the Bhagavad Gītā says. Even though imperfect,
you should continue to do your duties, according to your station in life.

Anjli: No, but this is a little different. The choice is between the
judgments arrived at by himself which he thinks are right or the
judgments of *sāttvic* people or the Scriptures.

Swāmiji: It is better to follow his own judgment, though imperfect, as
to what is right. If he lives somebody else's *dharma*, Bhagavad Gītā
says the judgment is very frightening and terrible because he is not
exhausting his *vāsanās*, nor is he able to live somebody else's

---

* "जानामि धर्मं न च मे प्रवृत्ति
जानामि अधर्मं न च मे निवृत्ति।
केनापि देवेन हृदिस्थितेन
यथा नियुक्तोऽस्मि तथा करोमि॥"

                                        - Duryodhana, in the Mahabharata.

judgment correctly, fully. To work in the field ordered by one's own *vāsanās*, the innate tendencies in the subconscious, is better, because in that case there is a chance of exhausting the existing *vāsanās*. When an individual strives in a field contrary to his existing tendencies, he not only fails to exhaust his *vāsanās*, but he also creates a new load of *vāsanās* in his temperament. One should follow the subjective tendencies even if they be defective. But at the same time we must try to courageously renounce all the demands that the objective world makes upon us from without. If there be an influx of wrong *vāsanās* within, the earlier we exhaust them though *Karma Yoga*— action without any ego or egocentric desire to enjoy its fruit—the quicker shall the load of existing *vāsanās* be lifted from our personality. When the load of *vāsanās* is reduced, our judgment will become purer and more in tune with the higher principles.

Free Will

Anjli: At every turn of our life we are faced with a choice, at any moment we could make a wrong judgment, and the whole responsibility of its consequences is on our shoulders. Sometimes one feels we are impelled to choose in a particular direction. Is the choice really ours? How free are we?

Swamiji: Man alone is the one animal who can, at each challenge in life, discriminate between the path of good and the path of evil. When man of his own accord refuses the blessings of the power of discrimination that his intellect is capable of, he is deliberately flouting his privilege as a human being. When one has thus of his own free will chosen to be only an animal, certainly nature will bless him only with the sorrows and limitations of the animal. It depends on how we cultivate and train the mind and intellect. If we tune them to the lower impermanent values of negativity, we become insensitive animals. Train them to think and act in terms of higher and permanent values of love, tolerance and mercy, we become cultured and perfected architects of our future.

Our whole future is based on how we act today. Life is a series of challenges. Moment to moment we are faced with decisions to do or not to do. Our intellect is called upon at each moment to evaluate independently and come to a judgment. Hence, no choice is the same as any other. With reference to this ever-changing pattern we are called upon moment to moment to make independent decisions to ascertain and to maintain our relationship with the external world. The wise and discriminating people at each juncture gently judge the various challenges that they face and determine never to swerve from the path of the good. The ignorant people, on the other hand, live like mules following the crowd and choosing the path of least resistance, motivated by the animal urges to satisfy the demands of the senses. Self-development is through self-effort. Man has been given the freedom to be good or to be vicious in his moment-to-moment contact with the external world. Certainly man does not have a complete and unlimited freedom over external circumstances. These external circumstances or environments in which he finds himself are the result of his earlier choices. Man has been preparing bit by bit a blueprint of his life by his choice of action. The edifice of external environment and inner impulses in which he finds himself is of his own making. And his present choice is within the limitation of that edifice.

Anjli: Which is more powerful then — *puruṣārtha,* free will, or *prārabdha,* destiny? Can we break away from a deterministic philosphy?

Swamiji: People misunderstand the real meaning of *prārabdha* when they take the word to mean all the failure, impotence, and weakness in them. If we are to be guided by this meaning there would be no room for self-improvement through self-effort. This is a defeatist mentality. That we have been given a limited freedom is the truth. For example, we cannot bend a piece of rail as it is, but supposing this rail-piece is beaten and made into a chain, the same rail becomes easily pliable. Similarly, when a cow is tied to a rope in the centre of a pasture, she is not free to graze the entire field, but she can move freely within the circle described by that rope.

At each moment of our life we are not only reaping the fruits of our past actions, but we are also creating the fruits of tomorrow. The past modified in the present alone is the future. There is no slavery, nor is there full freedom. There is limited freedom, which if intelligently used can redeem us from all enslavement. *What* we meet in life is *prārabdha — how* we meet it is *puruṣārtha.*

Meera: If according to the *Law of Karma* my freedom is limited, then is not my moral responsibility equally limited?

Swamiji: Yes, it is equally limited.

Meera: Could you elaborate?

Swamiji: The responsibility of a child is less than an adult's because his knowledge is less. As he grows up he comes to say "my responsibility is increased." Your responsibility becomes greater as you grow. As you become more and more grown up in knowledge, in your influence in the world, your moral responsibility becomes more. So moral responsibilities quantitatively increase.

Meera: When your freedom is limited by your own past actions, which you don't have control over now, and you find yourself in circumstances outside your entire control, then how morally responsible are you?

Swamiji: When you enter spiritual life, you are following *yoga* in order to exhaust your *vāsanās*. To the extent you unload them and get free within, your moral responsibility increases. Just as a *brāhmin* has more moral responsibility than a *sūdra*, a *sāttvic* man's responsibility is more than a *rājasic* or a *tāmasic* man's.

A Summing up

Anjli: In summing up all your answers upto now, would you say that though we do not refer every action to an ultimate standard because the stage of evolution varies from individual to individual, we do act in general with reference to immediate standards? These standards are set up by our station in life and constituted by the degree of mental purity in each one of us, and these help to lift us nearer to the final goal, which is identity with the Absolute. All immediate terms of reference like "motive," "means," "psychological reaction," and the standard of "happiness" that a man employs to judge an action to be right or wrong are interrelated and do not contradict one another. Since the final goal to be reached by man is a total sense of fulfilment or absolute happiness, any action that brings in its sum total reaction a sense of peace, fulfilment, and self satisfaction and leads us one step up the ladder of spiritual evolution is to be considered good.

The basis of ethics is action within the law of cause and effect, therefore we are the authors of our own destiny. The limitation of the environment in which we find ourselves is made by us by our past actions. Our present actions within that limitation will determine our future environment. The choice in the present is ours. The aim is to get out of the empirical hold of this law and onto the seat of the Absolute. No laws of action bind a man who has reached the final goal, the *Summum Bonum*, the absolute, intrinsic Good. Ethics ceases to be applicable only at this transcendental level where a person has found his identity with his real Self.

Swamiji: Yes. Perfect. But why are you breaking your head on this?!

PART II

RELIGION AND MORALITY

Its Relationship

Meera: Is there any relation between man's ethical norms and religious beliefs? Which depends on which? Ethical norms need not necessarily be based on religious beliefs.

Swamiji: Religion cannot exist without ethical norms. Ethics has value only with reference to the spiritual values or religious values. Without spiritual values, love could not be better than hatredness. Religion teaches that the whole creation is one, and thus our essential nature is to seek identity with everything.

All ethical principles, whether one recognizes religion or not, spring from religion. Religion here is meant in the larger sense of the term as rising above one's limited ego in dedication to a higher goal. Now, when one starts practising ethics, unless one has an ideal, a goal to surrender to and be dedicated to, one will not be able to stand against the temptations of the immediate pressures. Whenever I act from the egocentric standpoint, my action becomes immoral. Morality is to rise above the ego, and one can do it. Wherever one has an altar of dedication, that is called religion. The altar may be art, literature, politics, or one's own profession; whatever it is, it becomes a religion. "My profession is my religion." There are so many people who say that.

Influence on Behaviour

Meera: Religion tends to influence our behaviour greatly. Abraham's decision to sacrifice his son Isaac to prove his devotion to God, and Parasurām killing his mother were both religiously motivated. Admittedly, both are examples of great faith, but can we refer to them as great moral examples? Is it safe? There are countless examples of dominance of religion over ethics, of children being sacrificed to goddesses, etc.

Swamiji: In those cases, both Isaac and the mother were saved.

Meera: But the perpetraters did not know that when they performed the act.

Swamiji: The idea in the Paraṣurām story was only whether he should implicitly obey his father who was also his teacher. Paraṣurām's father asked him to chop off his mother's head. The son had no compunction. First obey and then complain. Paraṣurām obeyed first, and then the father said "I am pleased with you. I am going to bless you." " Sir, bless me, but my mother's head must be back again." It is something like the father shooting an arrow through the apple on the boy's head. What is his name?

Anjli: William Tell.

Swamiji: Yes. And the father did it. Was it morally right to do so just to save himself? No, the story is meant to bring out only the fact that even at that time he was so calm and serene and confident. •

Anjli: Paraṣurām also had full faith in his father, that he would bring his mother back to life.

Swamiji: Correct. When his father gave the order he never knew that his father was going to bless him. First implicit obedience to the teacher or the father is to be practised. There is no question of staying there and thinking. And as a result of that implicit obedience, he earned his blessing. Then he made use of it for the mother. The mother had sinned, and in order to exhaust the result of that sin the father ordered her death, knowing full well that the son would seek this boon.

Anjli: What about all the stories we read every day in the papers about children being sacrificed to some deity?

Swamiji: I don't believe them.

Anjli: It's happening every day.

Swamiji: That is what you read in the newspapers. Everything in print cannot be accepted. You have not taken the pleasure or the effort of going to that spot and making your own inquiries.

Anjli: One cannot doubt it every time.

Swamiji: It is doubtable. I doubt it. I don't think it will ever happen. Just now in the newspaper I read of a man who had been killing people for the last thirty years or so. More than forty to fifty people had already been killed when the FBI in America got wind of it. They started cleaning his place and they found ashes. The murderer saw he was about to be caught, and he took potassium cyanide and died. A man did it, actually did it. There was an FBI inquiry. We don't know why he killed, except that it was a psychological

aberration. Now when this happens in India, they say he was sacrificing
to the *Devi*.

Anjli: So acutally they are psychlogical cases?

Swamiji: Yes, psychological cases. The victim might have been a child or
a man, but they say it was a sacrifice and religion gets blamed. They are
all psychological cases. Religion is not to blame.

Divine Ordinance

Meera: Would it not be safer to separate religion from morality and make
moral sanction independent of divine injunction?

Swamiji: If you can do it, go ahead.

Meera: Does the rightness of an action depend upon divine ordinance,
or can an act be right in itself? Christianity and the Vedas both admit
āpta vākya, or religious testimony, as a valid source of knowledge.

Swamiji: Apta vākya is in reference to the experience of saints and sages
who have realized the Self and the knowledge they handed down after
the realization. It does not refer to ethical action, which comes within
the purview of rational reflection.

Trustworthiness of Instincts

Jyoti: As young people, we often act without consciously weighing the
motives and desired results. As we grow older there is more often a
sense of weighing alternatives. We feel naturally inclined to do something, but our rationality or long-term interest tells us to do something
else. Psychoanalysis tells us that we do not take enough notice of our
unconscious. To what extent should we trust our instincts? Is not the
unconscious really the more fundamental part of ourselves, whereas at
present our most powerful instinct is the animal instinct?

Swamiji: Yes, therefore presently we have to train our unconscious to
function better. Then we can depend upon instincts, that will be noble
instincts. At this moment our instincts are very impure. So if you live
according to the instincts in you, your instincts will be the whisperings
of your selfish ego. Never do that. But when you have practised for a
long period of time, living the higher values of life and following the
instructions of great masters or the Scriptures, that is, when you have
trained your unconscious, then when a situation comes, you can, to an
extent, depend on your inner voice. In order to purify our inner

instincts we follow moral rules and ethical principles. For a long period you live uncompromisingly those higher values. And then only, when they are chastened sufficiently to hear and reflect, then only could it become a medium   for the super-consciousness to function through.

In Pursuit of Higher Values

Anjli: I hope Swamiji does not think it too personal, but if Swamiji had not been able to persuade his father, would Swamiji have taken to *sannyās*, renunciation? Is it right to seek one's own greater good by causing unhappiness to those who love you? If the answer is "yes" on the grounds that it does greater good to the society afterwards, it must be remembered that when a person takes *sannyās*, he does not initially take this step for society, but for himself. If the answer is "no", how would you justify Siddhārtha, the Buddha, abandoning his wife and child?

Meera: Can one give up one's duty in the pursuit of a higher value?

Swamiji: Did not Rāma do it when he pursued a higher duty, the higher value of protecting the father's words? Did he not give up the smaller duty of serving his father?

In my case you know, that is the reason I wrote to my father, saying incase he said so, I will go and serve him. But I knew what was going to be my future, what it was that I wanted. "So then don't force me to get myself entangled in life. But if you wish I will come there and serve you all your lifetime. And I know what to do with my life." Luckily, he said "No, no, this is exactly what I also wanted to do, but I had not the courage. You do what I did not have the courage to do..."

Anjli: What about another person whose parents had said "no". Should that person take *sannyās*? Suppose he is their only son and they were against it, should he go ahead, do you think?

Swamiji: No. His time will come.

Imparting Values to Children

Meera: Do you think that strict moral training from a very early age will curb the urge to evil? What kind of moral education should be imparted to a child from the primary level, so that he will be spontaneously good and not have to go through repeated moral conflicts while making a choice?

Jyoti: How can we best express to our children the idea of genuine values so that they grow up with open minds, not with a once and for all acceptance but with the ability to sift and decide on right values? If we impart a vague sense of values they may grow up having no real sense of them at all. On the other hand, if we decide for them, they may be limited in their approach to values.

Swamiji: The first question is answered by the second question. The first question is: How are we to do it? The moral part only comes once the activity starts and we classify activities as moral and immoral. Now, how am I to make an individual to act morally? By giving him healthy values. Values of life determine how the individual reacts to the external world and finally expresses it.

Jyoti: How can one impart the values?

Swamiji: Values impartation must be started from the very beginning. Values are so subtle that even an elderly person will not be able to conceive the idea unless it is concretized in an individual acting those values in a given set of specific conditions. Thus Harish Chandra's story, when you relate it to the children, they understand the compelling situations. Harish Chandra's own son died, then the mother brought the body for cremation to that fellow who happened to be her husband who said, "Sorry, ten paise is the tax, you pay it." She said "I haven't got a pie." "Then get out of here. My master has fixed me here to collect the tax. Wait here. When the master comes in the morning you discuss it with him. If the master says he has no objection, the matter could be settled." So the truthfulness, the honesty of words, you know all these from the story alone. You may forget the story but the idea goes in. This is the method. In our modern education we don't give the children any ideal. Data is given but no ideal to pursue. Ideals must be given. The story is not for history, it is for imparting an ideal. Give it to them and they will always check whether their action was morally good or not, beautiful or not. These children will grow up and in their togetherness will constitute the society.

The social behaviour in any part of the world, in any period of time, will be the sum total work of the team of people that constitute the society. Each individual functions in the world outside ordered by, governed by his thoughts. The quality and the nature of the thoughts are determined by what values the individual respects. If the values respected by the individuals are wrong, the individual's activities can never be good. Similarly, the values entertained by the community or the society are wrong, their total behaviour will be only bringing more and more sorrow to them. Hence in the modern times we are insisting upon value based education. The healthy values, psychologically healthy for the individual and therefore healthy for the community have been experimented upon and given out as moral and ethical principles.

First, we have to conceive and understand and appreciate these values. Thereafter, a mere possession is not sufficient. Each individual should learn to live upto them. In order to impart these to our growing children there is no way other than concretizing these values through the heroic stories of people who have lived these values.... Hence the need for stories. The mythological stories of India are perfect and artistic examples on how to impart these values to children. Never can children's education be complete unless we impart to them a true appreciation of the eternal values of life and also help them to open up their sense of beauty and rythm, their astheticism and ethicism. That is the reason why we not only try to mold them with our stories of heroism and excellence in character but also give them a free choice to discover and develop their inner secret talents for music, dance, painting, etc. If has been found very rewarding in all our centres.

Do Values have Intrinsic or Extrinsic Worth? _____

Anjli: Do the values of life have intrinsic worth or do they have instrumental worth? In other words, is the value valuable in itself or is it as an instrument to achieving something else that a value is valuable?

Swamiji: A value is valuable only in relationship to achievements. It is instrumental. It is not absolute. Only *Brahman,* the Supreme Reality, has absolute value.

Anjli: You mean, *Brahman* is the only thing of intrinsic value?

Swamiji: The only intrinsic value. All others are instrumental or contributory to reaching that highest intrinsic value. By pursuing negative values you go away from Him. By pursuing positive values you go towards Him. So, values to be acquired by the seeker are only to take you to that instrinsic value, the absolute value that is *Brahman*.

Values of Life _____

Truthfulness

Anjli: Although each action in itself is relative, yet there are certain commandments, what we call values in life, that are recommended by all religions. For instance truthfulness. What makes speaking the truth valuable? Why is it advised as a general principle?

Swamiji: Truthfulness consists mainly in uttering a thought as it is actually perceived. Ordinarily, a liar is one who does not have the moral courage to express what he sincerely feels. This disparity between thought and words creates in his mind a habit to entertain a sort of "self-cancellation" of thoughts. This impoverishes the individual's mental strength, will power, and dynamism. Such an exhausted mental character is too weak thereafter to make any progress in life's pilgrimage.

Truthfulness in its essential meaning is not merely giving a verbal expression to one's honest feelings, but in its deeper import it is the attunement of one's mental thoughts to his or her intellectual convictions. Unless we are ready to discipline and marshal our thought-forces to the unquestioning authority of our own reason, chastened with knowledge, in the ensueing chaos within, we could not grow to realize the fuller unfoldment of our true and divine nature.

Charity

Anjli: Explain to us the value of charity?

Swamiji: Charity must come from one's sense of abundance. True charity springs from a sense of oneness between the giver and the recipient. Unless one is able to identify oneself with others, one will not feel the noble urge to share one's possesions with others. Thus charity is born out of a capacity to restrain one's instincts of acquisition and aggrandizement, and to replace these with the spirit of sacrifice.

In the name of charity many a thing is ordinarily done in society which destroys both the giver and the recipient. Therefore gifts should be given in accordance with certain ethical norms. Gifts should be given with faith. We can have faith only in what we understand to be right. Therefore charity is acceptable only when it toes the line of our independent, intellectual beliefs and convictions. Unless we are convinced of the nobility and unless we have come to a correct and independent judgment of the worthiness of the cause, charity should not be practised. Every benefactor has the right to inquire into the cause that he is trying to patronize.

Again, a miserly giving will not benefit either the giver or the receiver and, it is said in our Scriptures, having come to judge a cause as worthy, give it your entire patronage "Give in plenty, with both hands give." Also, charity must be given with modesty, avoiding feelings of egotism and vanity. It must be given with sympathy which comes from having surrendered to a higher altar. Sympathy generates love in us, and unless this love element predominates, compelling us to seek an identity with the cause, we will not spiritually evolve along the path of charity. Charity constricts the heart and obstructs human growth if it is not honeyed with the spirit of love and the joy of identification. Throwing fifty paisa (cents) to a helpless beggar and making him struggle to pick it up from the wayside dirt with his shrivelled, leprous fingers is no charity at all, however thick the giver may wear his caste-marks on his narrow forehead!!

Duty

Anjli: What is the importance of duty?

Swamiji: Religion is built upon duties and not upon rights. A civilization that is based upon "rights" must necessarily come to clamour and fight. The instincts of acquiring and hoarding, keeping and maintaining would develop in that society and ultimately upset the peace. On the other hand, a generation that has understood the value of performing duty will be trained to demand of life only chances to fulfil its duty. Duty therefore develops the spirit of giving, the urge to be charitable, and not the lust to hoard or the anxiety to keep.

Nonviolence

Anjli: What about nonviolence, or *ahimsa*?

Swamiji: *Ahimsa* in its spiritual import means never having cruel intentions. Noninjury is the spirit that should dominate all our motives. Our intentions should not be polluted by even a trace of cruelty or hatred. Harmlessness consists not so much in never causing physical injury to a being as in never comtemplating to do harm of any sort. Practising noninjury physically is impossible. To continue living, some kind of physical harm is unavoidable. But even while bringing about unavoidable disturbances around ourselves, if our motives are pure and clean, the harm so brought about is not regarded as injury. If you protect yourself against a robber in your own home or protest against aggressors, you are not transgressing *ahimsa*. To smash a serpent or a scorpion in your house is not an act of cruelty. On the contrary, to allow these to flourish in the name of nonviolence is weakness sanctioned only by a misinterpreted culture.

Thus, noninjury is a value of life to be applied at the level of our motives. Our motives must be noninjurious and pure. This purity of intention can arise only out of a deep sense of oneness with the Lord's creation and compassion toward all beings, good and bad alike.

Gentleness in Speech

Anjli: It is very difficult to never get angry. How far must one control one's temper?

Swamiji: One should develop a capacity to check anger as it arises. It will be almost unnatural to expect the mind to become incapable of anger. But no emotion should be allowed to overwhelm us to a degree where it renders us helpless.

Anjli: Sometimes temper leads to very harsh speech.

Swamiji: The ugliness or beauty of the tongue is ordered by the personality behind. A shattered entity will seek self-gratification in malicious and harsh words, and the soft tongue can often become more devastating than the most destructive missile. A seeker trying to reach a fuller and more exhaustive self-expression should develop such inward harmony that his speech echoes the fragrance of his soul. A speech with softness of tone, clarity of expression, honesty of conviction, power of bringing a clear picture in the listener's mind, overflowing with sincerity, devotion, and love becomes the very quality of the speaker's personality. To develop, therefore, a habit of such speech would be to unconsciously train and discipline one's inner equipment.

Forbearance

Anjli: How should one meet the pinpricks and also the major setbacks of life?

Swamiji: With forbearance. The ability to live patiently through minor or major physical or mental inconveniences is forbearance — a subtle boldness that is displayed by a person while facing adversity. When an individual daringly confronts life, he cannot always expect happy situations, favourable circumstances, and conducive opportunities. When encountering opposition, many a weak individual feels dejected and is tempted to leave the field of work when it is only half done. Many lose the chance of achieving their goal and desert the field of action almost at the moment that victory is imminent.

In order to stick to our convictions, we need spiritual energy to nurture and nourish our fatigued morales. This inner energy welling up in a well-integrated personality is called fortitude or forbearance. The strength of faith, conviction in the goal, consistency of purpose, vivid perception of the ideal, and a bold spirit of sacrifice cultivated diligently all form the source from which fortitude trickles down to remove our exhaustion and despair.

Purity

Anjli: Isn't outer cleanliness related to inner purity?

Swamiji: The word cleanliness indicates not only the inner purity—thoughts and motives—but it also suggests the purity of environment, and cleanliness of habit and personal belongings. As a result of an over-emphasis on subjective purity today, we find in Indian society an utter neglect of external purity. Clean clothes and civic habits have both become rare in our society.

Outer cleanliness is, to a large measure, a reflection of the inner condition. A disciplined person with education and culture alone can maintain systematic order and cleanliness around him. One who is aspiring to reach perfection will necessarily be so well-disciplined physically that he will be clean both in his relationship with others and in the condition of his belongings around him. It is well known that the condition of a person's table and the cleanliness of his apparel give a great insight into the mental nature, discipline, and culture of that man. In the Scriptures great emphasis has been laid on physical purity, not only in the person but also in his contacts with the world. Without external purity, internal purification will be but a vague dream, an idle hope, a despairing vision.

At the same time, no amount of external discipline can supply a person with the positive dynamism that is the very core in moral living. A man must live the highest values of life. Then he can burst forth with a positive glow of righteousness and bathe the entire generation in the light of truth and virtue—virtue that implies honesty of intentions and purity of motives.

Service

Anjli: Is service of mankind an important value?

Swamiji: Dedicated work is a means for the inner purification of one's *vāsanās*. Though the goal is Self-realization, which is realized through the path of renunciation, stages of progress from "animal-man" to "God-man" are through an intermediary stage called "man-man."

The Upaniṣads glorify service as the highest pinnacle of right living. Dedicated and noble work alone can polish an individual to a state of true culture and right discipline. To those who know what service is, work is not a slavery or drudgery but is the joy of life. Man is not born to revel in idleness.

Vedanta has never permitted escapism, although many uninformed people contend that it does. The earliest Upaniṣads emphasize that one who cannot live the noble life of renunciation and self-restraint must strive to fulfil one's desires through honest means; teaching oneself to live in the service of man and in the glorification of the Lord. Such actions involving service of mankind are necessary to prepare a student for the highest flights in meditation.

Actions do not cling to one who intensively plunges into life, eager and anxious to meet its new challenges, at every turn keeping truth and purity as one's standards. Such a one is living an entire lifetime in the spirit of paying homage to the Lord, detached from the ego-sense or from the anxiety for the result of those actions. When all activities, whether social, economic, political, or domestic, are pursued in an attitude of detachment, they can never bind the person by their results.

The highest prayer in the world is service, the greatest devotion is loving the people around, and the noblest character trait is divine compassion for all living creatures.

Contentment

Anjli: Whenever a desire gets satisfied, one feels happy. But after a while, we always want something more. It seems as if nothing is enough.

Swamiji: Greed is due to the erosion of one's mental strength and inner peace when desires are more and more satiated. When a desire gets fulfilled, an insatiable thirst for more and more joy holds the individual, and this endless appetite ruins the mental strength and saps dry the personality-vitality. Greed is a sense of dissatisfaction constantly pursuing and poisoning the sense of satisfaction that we have already experienced. In an indisciplined man, there can be no satisfaction at any time. He is unhappy even when his desires are satisfied because his appetite for enjoyment is sharpened and he hungers for more. If the desires are throttled the disappointment brings him a thought storm of anger, and he suffers the consequent wretchedness.

Contentment with whatever has come to one as one's just share is the motto of all serious seekers. To endlessly entertain and satisfy the demands of life would be an unending game, for the mind has a knack of breeding its own demands very quickly. The policy of contentment is the only intelligent attitude to be taken up by sincere seekers or else there will be no time to·seek, to strive for, and to achieve the divine goal of life. Self-integration is the reward promised for all faithful pursuits.

Equipoise

Anjli: Often one gets shaken by happenings around and then loses the ground that has been gained. One's equilibrium gets upset every now and then.

Swamiji: Equipoise is a state of mental equilibrium that comes when one has unshakeable intellectual foundations and the mental capacity to soar to the highest pinnacles of greater visions. When a person raises himself into greater ambits of spiritual vision, his mind will no longer entertain any agitations at the ordinary level of likes and dislikes. None of the happenings at the level of the mind and intellect can be of any serious consequence to a person who is trying to detach from the dualistic experiences and who has learned the art of drawing inspiration from something beyond.

Detachment

Anjli: How can a mind detach itself from the happenings and situations around?

Swamiji: Detachment should not be understood as a running away from situations in life. This we can never do; an escapist is never a champion in the spiritual path. Ignorant of this fact, many have wrecked their spiritual unfoldment by merely running away from sense-objects and comforts. Detachment is an intelligent attitude to life and the environment. We cannot avoid the world. The world will impinge upon us whether we wish it or not. We have to be in the world so long as we live in the present plane of consciousness. There is no escape from perceptions, emotions, or thoughts.

Detachment is a mental attitude intelligently maintained toward objects and beings around. Mere understanding of the pain-ridden nature of the finite world is not sufficient; this understanding must be completely assimilated by constant thinking and continuous realization. Through intelligent and awareful experiments in our own life, we can build up an ever increasing realization that detachment pays a high dividend. The knowledge so gained, the conviction so gathered as a result of our own personal experience, is what is meant by the term, "continuous realization."

In fact, the objects and beings that constitute the world cannot bring any storm into us. The shattering shocks in life, not only the tragic events but even the day-to-day pinpricks in life, are all received by us only because we are making wrong contacts with the world around us. Our reaction to the environment will depend upon our mental evaluation of it on and our inner nature at that particular moment. If our inward nature can be arranged, and continuously held in that arrangement, so as to make us react with the world positively, then we have discovered the secret of living in peace with the world, independent of its happenings. This arrangement in one's inner nature is called detachment, and a personality that has developed detachment becomes a nonconductor of the shocks in life.

Such a person is tranquil, efficiently intelligent, and peacefully serene at all times.

This glorious spirit of detachment cannot be practised in a sequestered place where there are no temptations and no challenges around. No one can learn swimming on the dry banks of a river. One must live in this world fully and enthusiastically and learn the art of doing so in a spirit of intelligent detachment.

Meditation

Anjli: What must one do to be able to meditate?
Swamiji: First of all you must expose yourself to aloneness. When a person is left alone, he start thinking of the higher reality—about

death, life, soul, God and the mystery of all. Man must strive to
seek the absolute Good, which is a state of being, apprehended
within oneself.

Anjli: Does the absolute and intrinsic Good really exist? Can one see
it? Does meditation help in a practical way?

Swamiji: It is not perceived by the senses but it does exist. The fact that
the earth is round and moves, is not seen, but is true. The sky is blue,
the sunset is golden—they are seen but false. Energy in the atom,
vitality in the sun, gravitational force—not seen, but true. Double
moon, mirage waters, dream and hallucinations seen, but false. The
world we see, but it is not true, the truth we see not, but it is true.

To achieve the state of conscious being, the physical, mental, intellectual and spiritual personalities of a person must all be blended
into one harmonious whole. Meditation is the technique of achieving
this harmony. It is the highest spiritual discipline. Through meditation a person comes to experience peace within and without.
Internecine wars between desires end. Conflicts between duties no
longer wreck his nerves. His mind is able to view life as a whole. He
will always meet with success, for his meaningless flutterings and the
consequent dissipations have stopped. He directs his potentialities
with a concentration that cannot be baulked.

Observe the result of concentration all around you in the world. The
sun's rays coverging on a point through a focusing lens would burn
the thing on which they are concentrated. All successful professionals
owe their success to single-pointed efforts. Thoughts of problems
yield to undivided attention. Application of a divided mind brings
about indifferent results. Every person is a potential genius. Most of
us are able to use only an insignificant part of our infinite potentialities.
We have unlimited powers, which we have not learned to tap and
make use of. It is a question of rediscovering ourselves.

The mind is ever busy fluttering from one object to another. The flow
of thoughts is ceaseless. Obviously, before the mind can be made
to concentrate on anything, it must be cultivated. The intellect should
assert its mastery over the mind and order it to stop all thoughts
except the thought of the common denominator. By assiduous practice, the mind can learn to think of only one thing at a time. Such a
mind would indeed be a force to be reckoned with. Having become
conscious of its true nature, such a mind would not be disturbed by
either passing sorrows or ephemeral joys. Prosperity cannot spoil it
nor can adversity degrade it. Realization of the Supreme Goal of
life would give a new edge to life, and all the passing shows of the

world would appear in their stark nakedness, stripped of their power
to delude. All curtains would lift before the penetrating gaze of a
mind thus established in Pure Consciousness through regular meditation. Shorn of all complexes, it would no more be assailed by
doubts and fears.

Be regular in meditation. Be sincere. Be pure. Meditation can never
fail. It will ever be a success. Failures in meditation bring greater
gains than success in life. Meditate - meditate - meditate, and —
meditate. Sincerity and regularity are the secrets of success in meditation.

A Summing Up

Anjli: In summing up, Swamiji, you have said that all ethical principles
spring from religion, whether we recognize the goal as God or
Goodness or any other altar of dedication higher than ourselves.
Implicit obedience to ethical principles helps one to greater good,
and that certain antisocial acts attributed to religion are only psychologically perverted cases. Divine ordinance is a valid source of
knowledge of Reality because such a knowledge is experiential and
outside the capability of the intellect. Ethics, however, comes within
the purview of rational reflection, and therefore morality has to be
constructed individually depending on various factors and ethical
values. If one's dedication is to a higher ideal, one will demonstrate
positive and right values in life, thereby sharpening one's moral
sensitivity and improving the quality of behaviour and feelings toward
mankind. Individual development takes place by cultivating the
higher values of life which you have enumerated and giving reasons
why these values are valuable. Swamiji has also shown the importance
of guiding children and a simple method of imparting values and
ideals to them.

An intense session on Vedantic philosophy in Zürich

*"Man has been preparing
bit by bit a blue print of his life
by his choice of action.
The edifice of external environment
and inner impulses,
in which he finds himself,
is of his own making,
while his present choice
is within the limitation
of that edifice."*

The one and the many — at a philosophical camp in France

"Only he who has learned to love
at the altar of God
can truly love society,
otherwise even in love for society
you portray your vanity and selfishness.
When an individual enters the field of social work
or national service
without surrendering his ego
at a higher altar,
he does not always strive
in a true cooperative spirit."

An outdoor session in the Redwoods, California

*"The values that you uphold in life
determine the quality of thoughts;
the quality of thoughts
will determine in turn
the quality of actions."*

Loneliness perspires and aloneness inspires. Swamiji caught in an inspired mood in Kenya.

"Expose yourself to aloneness.
When a person is left alone
he start thinking
of the higher reality,
about death
life
soul
God
and the mystery
of all."

PART THREE

SPECIFIC ENQUIRIES ON SOCIAL ETHICS

Social Conscience _____

Jyoti: Why is it that in India we have not been able to widen our spheres of morality? We are concerned, loving parents, wives, and children. Could we at the same time be impervious to the needs of people who do not fall into our immediate sphere of interest?

Swamiji: That is worded very confusingly. Never mind! In India now, people are very moral individually. But in community living, there is no morality. People need training. Because of long centuries of foreign rule, people have become utterly selfish, always with a self-preservation instinct and a sense of insecurity. Now we have to train ourselves to live socially and have the social feeling that we are all one. Then there will be some social morality. This we have to teach ourselves.

Jyoti: In a country like India or anywhere else where we see so much misery around us, is it not self centred to be interested only in our own personal spiritual development? Like any other discipline, only more so, spiritual development takes time and effort. Would that time and effort not be more valuably used in helping others? Perhaps this is the only ethical way of trying to achieve *mokṣa*, liberation.

Swamiji: Firstly, you are saying that first-aid is more important than curing as the latter will take a long period of time. So let us give first-aid only. When you say economic misery and all that, what we are trying to do is find the cause of that misery. The cause lies in the unchastened thoughts of the mind. If everybody were to love each other, all this misery would not be there. We are very selfish individually, and misery is there. What the politician is trying to do is a superficial facelifting of the society. That does not cure. By changing the bandage the wound will not be healed. We are trying to heal the wound by developing spiritually and thus helping others.

Anjli: "I give no alms to satisfy the hunger of my brother, but to fulfil and accomplish the will and command of my God" said Sir T. Broune as a fitting illustration to Kant's stringest doctrine of duty for duty's sake. Would Swamiji say that an action is good when it is done only out of a sense of duty and without feeling of pity or sympathy or love? Or is that action better which is motivated by love or sympathy and not merely by a sense of duty?

Swamiji: You are not talking of feelings but of sentiment. If his dedication is to God and his love is for God, he has feeling. He says, "I am doing it for God, not for this particular individual." When one acts for an individual it is out of sentiment. "I am doing it because he is my brother. Had he been my enemy. I would not have done it. Let him hang or die." If, on the other hand, my love is for a higher Being whose children these are, I rise above my own personal prejudices, isn't it so?

Anjli: Out of feeling for God, a sense of duty arises for others?

Swamiji: A feeling for God or any goal higher than himself. The higher his goal or love, the more beautiful his action. "I love my wife and children, therefore I am doing it". The feeling of love may be there, but the act is still selfish. If his action is motivated by concern for society, e.g. a larger love, his action is of a higher order. Did Broune understand it like that? I don't think so.

Anjli: He said it as an illustration of Kant's principle of moral reason because Kant's doctrine is very stringent and very rational. Kant did not think any conduct is virtuous if it rests solely on feeling. Although Kant insisted that duty must not be done from inclination, he never denied that it may be done with inclination. He would bow down to duty even if there were no love or sympathy involved in the action. The criticism of Kant is that there should be love and sympathy in action for it to be considered good.

Swamiji: But then what Kant is trying to do is *His* duty only. His command he obeys not as commanded by Him but because of his love for Him. Just like I obey the command of my child and my wife, because of my love for them.

Anjli: When my goal is larger, the act of helping others would be with love and sympathy?

Swamiji: When you are doing it as a duty will it not be with love? Where there is no love how could there be a sense of duty?

Anjli: The love is only for God, but not for humanity as such.

Swamiji: Love for God cannot be restricted to God as an individual only. It also expresses itself as love for the community, love for the country, love for the Lord in all.

Anjli: Suppose a man obeys a religious commandment that one should give charity and so he gives it, but not because he feels any sympathy or love for the people who are suffering. Wouldn't it be better to give out of a feeling of sympathy or even pity rather than just out of a sense of duty generated by my love for something else?

Swamiji: Pity is a sentiment, a cheap emotion. And underlying it is the thought. "Lucky I am not in that condition. Let me give something."

Jyoti: Is it possible to sacrifice to God who is intangible and unknown without having developed a capacity to love and identify with human beings?

Swamiji: We already know how to love human beings. In fact we don't really love them. We only love ourselves. Our love at this moment is utterly selfish and desire-prompted. When love is defiled by desire, it becomes lust. Love for the Lord is where we can develop pure love. When our desire for worldly possessions is eliminated, we can learn to love God. Only he who has learned to love at the altar of God can truly love society, otherwise even in love for society you portray your vanity and selfishness. When an individual enters the field of social work or national service without surrendering his ego to a higher altar, he does not always serve in a true cooperative spirit. In spite of very many of the leaders and workers striving hard for the upliftment of their country, we find that the world of our age is far short of peace, plenty, and prosperity. When a man of this type reaches a field of activity, in spite of his vociferous claims to selfless service, he is incapable of it because of the very nature of his personality and character. Such friends of society can perform social service in name only. Therefore, when entering the field of social activity all work should be surrendered to a higher altar as that brings about purification of the mind. The Lord alone is the highest altar and work done for the love of Him alone is true unselfish work.

Jyoti: Can one really love an abstract God, who seems to be only a "dry" state of consciousness?

Swamiji: Knowingly or unknowingly everybody loves it. One only wonders how one could love this "dry" state of consciousness. I run after things and people that bring me joy, believing that these give me satisfaction. I love my son only so long as he gives me happiness. It is a fact that everybody is selfish. But we misunderstand our self as the "perceiver feeler -thinker" entity, and this results in our activities being so vulgar. But when we understand that "I am the Self" then our "sell-fish" activities become "Self-ish" with a capital S. That Self is the the most lovable. All our activities are directed towards that Self, whose nature is total happiness which consciously or unconsciously man is always seeking. It is not a "dry" state of consciousness.

Euthanasia

Anjli: In the case of a patient suffering from an incurable disease such as cancer, would mercy killing be justified when the patient himself wants it?

Swamiji: Knowledge is to be used only in the service of mankind, and not to extend suffering. In certain cases in which our knowledge is limited and we know there is no other remedy available, mercy killing may be justified. It is not the killing that is important, as I told you earlier; it is the motive behind the action. There should be a council of wise men from the medical profession who could meet and decide whether in a particular case and in their branch of knowledge there is any remedy. All of them would have to agree. Then the individual could be allowed to die. It would not be killing. In fact it is not to be said that it is killing, rather it is not contributing to the continuation of the individual's sorrows.

Anjli: The other day in your talk you mentioned that one could withdraw medicines in such cases, but could one do something to put an end to the suffering altogether?

Swamiji: I am not asking you to inject and kill—No! Only withdraw the medicines.

Anjli: Suppose after the withdrawal of medicines the person continues to linger on...

Swamiji: It can't be helped. It must be allowed. We being religious people, we must surrender unto Him. Let the Lord cure the patient or let Him make him suffer where we are not contributing with our knowledge to lengthen the disease. The mercy killing is the mercy of the Lord, not your mercy. We leave it to God's mercy. Maybe the patient is required to go through the experience and for that purpose he has been made a vegetable. If he lingers as a vegetable, you and I, the family people or members of the community, are duty bound to watch over him and ensure that no harm comes to him from outside. Let nature take its own course.

Abortion

Meera: Is abortion justified in the Hindu ethical code?

Swamiji: If abortion means taking the life of a foetus, it is not allowed. No religion allows it. But the Hindu masters have been observing more exhaustively and they came to the conclusion that it is only after many weeks of conception that the feotus becomes charged with an individuality. Before that it has no independent life of its own. The individual life comes into it only after some time. In the Hindu Code, if the woman is pregnant for three months, then the child in the womb is considered as a member of the family. In the joint-family system, the mother gets two shares, one for the foetus and one for herself.

Anjli: At twevlve weeks it is a distinguishably formed foetus.

Swamiji: But it is not conscious. The subtle body consisting of the mind, intellect, and past impressions enters only after twelve weeks or so. Until then it is only existent, *sat.* The consciousness, *cit,* comes afterwards.

Anjli: Medical photography has shown life-reaction in feotuses. Even plants display life and sensitivity and they are not as highly evolved.

Swamiji: Not only plants, even your dead body has life; that is why worms come out of it! But the mind and intellect is not conscious in that body. Similarly the mind-intellect enters a body only after twelve weeks or so. Until then it is a physical shape which is growing with no conscious reaction. The reactions they display are instinctive ones. Till about ninety days we consider it only as a tumour-like growth with no individuality.

Sati

Anjli: What is your opinion about *sati?*

Swamiji: Never ask a swami his opinion! A swami has no opinion. It is like asking a scientist his opinion about the sub-nuclear theory. He can only tell you the theory. So then, *sati* was practised ages ago, especially by the Rajputs. It was a tribute paid to the vulgar conquerors, who used to rape the Hindu widows. So these women thought it better to protect their honour and die, rather than to be subjected to dishonour. In the olden days, when a woman became a widow, it was not like nowadays, to remarry—his fourth and her third. Our Hindu *dharma* is so designed that it meant that it was time for her to turn inward. She would dress simply in white as she used to dress not for the public, but for her husband. And then she concentrated on looking after the household duties, as there was the joint family and not just husband, wife, and children. She had no social responsibilities, she did not have to attend any death ceremonies or marriage functions. Even if she was young, she understood that it was time for her to give up her extrovertedness and turn inward: as the Lord had taken away her sensuous *vāsanās* by taking her husband away, because He gives the field that you need for exhausting your *vāsanās*. So she would understand this and devote her time to prayer and worship. She turned more and more inward. Only after her household duties were over would she bathe, do *pūja*, worship, and eat, but not for taste. And thus she lived. *Sati* was practiced only when the women had to protect their honour. Now, it is not necessary any longer, and there was an outcry, and a bill against *sati* was passed, and so it was stopped. Now it is not needed or necessary.

Anjli: It is a shame that some people still advocate the practice of *sati* and want to live in the past. You have said that a culture dies if it refuses to change with the times.

In the Grey Areas of Choice

Indecision

Anjli: What if the intellect could not decide and come to a judgment about the course of action. In the grey areas of choice it is difficult to distinguish black from white. What should one do at such a juncture?

Swamiji: Why are you afraid? With whatever data is before you, go ahead and choose an action and carry it through. Even if the action chosen turns out to be a mistake, what does it matter? What do a few mistakes matter in one's long span of life? From the experience of the mistakes learn to discriminate more keenly. Don't be afraid to act. While doing the action if you realize it is a mistake, don't become indecisive again and leave the action. Continue with the action and tell the mind: "Now you suffer! You chose it, you suffer." and thereby learn to evaluate actions correctly and develop discrimination.

Error or Sin?

Anjli: Sometimes one acts for happiness but the result is sorrow in one's mental reaction. How does one differentiate between an immoral action and a mistake?

Swamiji: We only call such an act a mistake in order to soften it, but it is immoral. Mistake is only for those who say that "I knew it was bad. I don't know why I did it.", "I did it when I was much too hallucinated by the moment." Instead of calling it a mistake, call it an error of judgment. Then it softens a little more. And it is a fact too. Why were we not able to judge properly? Because of the lust in us. Therefore if sorrow comes out of it I shall receive it with both hands, knowing full well that the Lord is punishing me so that *antahkarana śuddhi,* inner purity, will come. Is it not? And if one does the wrong act once or twice consciously, the third time he will not do it.

Anjli: My next question is related to the earlier one. Suppose you do something and get caught. You react and say "I should not have done it." But you feel it was mistake only because you got caught. Had you not got caught you would not have reacted and admitted it as a mistake, you would have continued to think you did the right thing.

Swamiji: If you think after the action that you did nothing wrong, then you did the right thing. You have not done any wrong. Maybe you are not sensitive enough to feel it; if so, to you it is not a sin. To an animal, killing another animal is not a sin. For a man it could be a sin, the reason being that man is more sensitive. In the evolutionary ladder the ethical and moral rules are not common to all. So that which is a sin to a *brāhmin* may not be a sin to a *kṣatriya.* Even if a *brāhmin's* own life is in danger he is not supposed to kill, not even in self-defense. Why should he save himself, when for the rest of his life he will be feeling the guilt.

Anjli: Not even in self defense?

Swamiji: No! When Kapalika, a tribal, asked for the head of Adi Śankara to be offered in sacrifice, what did Śankara say? He said "Did you ask me for my head? Come tomorrow early morning because it is not safe for you now. You may get my head but you will not be able to go with it, because that Sureṣvaracarya must be somewhere here. He is terrible when guarding me. So come early morning, tomorrow. You can quietly take it away then." Śankara could never say "no" to anybody and society could demand anything from him.

Fall in the Value System

Anjli: To some people, the regret that "I should not have done it" never comes. In some Indian schools, for instance, cheating nowadays is considered normal; the teachers often help children to cheat so that the school as a whole fares better than other schools. Is such an action to be considered right on the part of children since the teachers themselves encourage it? This example, also relates to corruption in general, as most people are insensitive to it and it is to be found at all levels. Even the people who ought to be setting an example are indulging in it.

Swamiji: That is why I have recently started saying in my talks that in my country now there is no corruption. Today you can't call it corruption. Twenty years ago, yes, you could. Today many don't consider it as such. It has become a way of life. Their sensitivity is so dullened that at this moment what they are doing is not wrong to them. Just as when a drunken fool calls us names or abuses us, we walk away with a smile because when he comes to his senses he will apologise. In fact he may not even remember!

Anjli: So this sort of a thing, this sort of an action is not wrong from his individual point of view.

Swamiji: Standpoint. But it is a danger to the society.

Anjli: It is wrong from the standpoint of an ideal society, but not from the individual's?

Swamiji: From the individual's no, if he is really not sensitive. But those individuals are to be punished. You have to slowly make them sensitive. Through punishment, sorrow, and tears alone will sensitivity increase. Or else, the danger is that the whole society will collapse. It is something like a deadly disease, for instance, a leper is an honest man I admit, but leprosy is what will spread all over.

Anjli: So the cheating by students is to be considered wrong by others? But isn't ethics concerned only with people who are the doers themselves?

Swamiji: At this moment the students have not done any crime. But from the social worker's standpoint they have to catch them and punish them vigorously. Otherwise, in the long run society will not survive. By the time these children come of age there will be no society for them to live in and enjoy.

Anjli: The value system has to be raised.

Ethical consideration in Politics and Economics

Anjli: People, especially politicians, who are not always guided by a truly unbiased judgment are often guided by party policies to promulgate absurd laws and judgments. When in doubt, what should one do?

Swamiji: One should follow the advice of wise people in society who are the accredited champions of our culture. A wise man should be a man capable of independent thinking and correct judgment.

He must be one who is not merely secular in his concept of things, but he has respect for the sanctity of the sacred. He must not only be a man of independent, unbiased judgment and should be truly religious, with nothing to gain, but he must also be a man with full freedom to express his ideas. Such fearless men of dedication firmly established in their ideas and stoutly indepen dent, are the true guides of our culture, and you may follow them whenever there is doubt regarding either your action or your conduct.

Meera: When the moral convictions of a minority conflict with those of the majority, how is one to decide who is right? One cannot disregard this question as being political because ideally one's political decisions should be influenced by moral codes.

Swamiji: I think you should live up to your convictions in such cases, because in the Taittiriya Upaniṣad these methods are explained:

(a) Do as the Scriptures say. Incase the Scriptures are silent about the situation:

(b) Do as the other cultured people are doing. If that is not so:

(c) Ask your *guru*, or if the *guru* is not there:

(d) Close your eyes and ask yourself and live according to your own conviction. Perhaps you may make a mistake. Morally perfect you cannot be. One can only strive for it. Ultimately, morality is only realizing Him.

Anjli: Is it one's moral duty to overthrow a tyrannical and corrupt regime?

Swamiji: If you have the temperament of a *Kṣatriya*, yes. But if you have the temperament of a *brāhmin*, a *vaiśya* or a *śūdra*, you have no right. "Castes" are determined by temperament.

Anjli: But a *brāhmin* may fight injustice with other means, by his speech, etc. and not necessarily with arms.

Swamiji: Then it is not removing a corrupt regime. He is educating the people; that is his job, which he should do. Where there is immorality or corruption or tyranny, he must make the individuals understand what is going on, and what is right and what is not. But he himself does not enter the fray.

Anjli: What about the other two classes, *vaiśyas* and *śūdras*?

Swamiji : What about lawyers? Can a lawyer detect and decide my illness? He does not have the special knowledge, that is all. Only a doctor can decide. Similarly, a work or duty allocated to the *kṣatriya* suits only him. *Kṣatriya* does not mean by birth, no! It means one who has got the restlessness of mind that makes it impossible for him to stay in a compromising situation. He is one who does not care for the consequences. His job is to fight. He must do it. Or else, the world will be too quiet!

Anjli: Suppose you have certain convictions and in following them it may disintegrate the society, even then should you live up to them?

Swamiji: Yes, always live up to your convictions. You have come into this world to live your life according to your convictions. Disunity may happen, when has it not happened in the history? But you have to live up to your convictions.

Anjli: Is it morally acceptable to defect from one's country if one does not agree with the prevailing political system?

Swamiji: No. Never should you leave your motherland. You have a duty towards it. The law of nature will never make a mistake; it is not accidental that you are born under particular circumstances, in a particular place. You need it for your development. If you walk away from the place of your birth into another plan, you are committing a kind of physical suicide. Just as when you are in trouble and want to commit suicide, you are trying to escape from a certain discipline that nature is putting you through. Anybody can walk out of a hospital. Nobody would stop him, only he would be walking away from a certain discipline that is necessary for him. The doctor is putting him on medicine and on a restricted diet because of his condition, to help him overcome the disease. It is momentarily inconvenient, maybe painful, but if he walks out he carries the disease into the streets, into the world. He would be a threat to others and to himself. So, you have to live in your own country. It is possible to leave it as a strategy. You may temporarily move out in order to fight the system, improve the system from outside. But a better way is not by moving out physically but by detaching, which is also a movement. Moving physically out of the country and defecting, giving out secrets that have been entrusted to you is immoral; it is wrong.

Anjli: Would it be considered selfish to claim one's just rights in money matters, or should one give in to the other person just to avoid unpleasantness?

Swamiji: It all depends upon the conditions and situation. If the other fellow is making a fool of you, don't yield your right to him. Teach him it is not worthwhile. If the other person is in trouble and you can afford it, don't pressurize him. Money is not everything.

Anjli: If the tax laws in a country are so stringent that people are forced to make money through various loopholes in the law to maintain a standard of living, would this be called an infringment of business ethics?

Swamiji: When the situation is so choking and taxation abominably high, people will automatically do it. It becomes not a question of morals but a question of survival. Business as an institution or as an individual has to survive. Unintelligent laws bring about this moral problem. When the problem comes, an average man will succumb to immorality readily. It takes a hero to stay honest in those circumstances and suffer for the sake of the general law. But such people will be only a handful, in any community, at any period of history, so intelligent governors should see that the laws are not stringent.

Sri Rāma's Dilemma

Anjli: Lord Rāma may have loved Sita dearly and sacrificed his own love for what is said to be democratic rule. But is it ideal democracy or ideal kingship to dole out injustice to one individual who is in the right, in this case his own wife, in order to appease a mob especially when Rāmāyana was written for the common man to make philosophical and ethical concepts easy to understand? Please, Swamiji, don't answer this question from the level of philosophic symbolism, that Lord Rāma represents the highest Self in man, the *Atman* and Sita represents the mind, but please answer it from the ethical standpoint and from the standpoint of justice.

Meera: In other words, can you sacrifice an individual to illustrate a general principle?

Swamiji: Here Rāma is the ideal man. All through Rāma's life we find the author using Rāma to express the ideal son, ideal brother, ideal husband, ideal enemy, ideal friend. Now here is an ideal king. Even with his wife, even though the king loves her dearly and knows fully well that she is honest and pure, but because the public wants it, he has no will other than the public's.

Anjli: But suppose it was someone else's wife, and he knew that the person was innocent, would he have made the same judgment?

Swamiji: Yes, he would have. And he did it.

A *śūdra* was doing *tapas* (intense austerities) by tying his feet to the branch of a tree with his head down in perpetual *sirsāsan* (head stand). He was doing *tapas*. The public rose against him saying that he had no right to do it. Rāma went there, and without any compunction cut his head off. After all, a *sūdra* was not supposed to do *tapas*. This is quoted very often against Rama.

Anjli: I do not know the story.

Swamiji: Sambuka, I think is his name. From Rāma's point of view, he was giving *mokṣa*. Slain by Rāma himself, here means, killing the ego.

Anjli: But from the social viewpoint it must have been to prevent power that accrues from concentration and austerities to come to someone who might not wield it justly. But that is digressing. Why should Rāma be dictated to by the public? Really speaking, Rāma was not demo-cratically chosen. He was the king. It was a monarchy, he alone should have been responsible for deciding and not the people.

Swamiji: In those days in India, democracy was under the kingship of those who lived with the democratic spirit. Although the kingship came to one because he was the son of his father and it was thus handed down because of birth, when a king came to the throne, he always lived with democratic values.

Anjli: In Sitā's case, it is as if the judge knew she was innocent but the jury pronounced her guilty!

Ethical Lapses during the Mahābhārata War _____

Anjli: Lord Krishna has been criticized for advising Arjuna to kill Karna against the war rules, for advising Yudhistara to tell a lie, and other such actions during the Mahābhārata war. One justification often given is that the enemy had been unfair and cruel on many more occasions before. For instance, they cheated at dice, ill -treated Draupadi and killed the defenseless Abhimanyu. Do two wrongs make a right? If you say that it is to show that war breeds such ill after-effects, still one does not expect 'sreṣtha puruṣas', ideal persons, to set such examples, especially in a great moral epic.

Swamiji: If a sanitary inspector entered a sewage canal to clean it, he would become soiled, and on coming out he would have to take a bath to become clean. Similarly, war is dirty. It brings out the worst in everybody. At the war front, you cannot go and say that you are a *brāhmin* and will speak only truth. If you want to do that then get out of the war. Go to the caves of the Himalayas. Don't come anywhere near the battlefield. Likewise in politics, all activities conducive to a goal are justified, the means are justified because of the goal in war.

Anjli: But why two standards, one for war and one for peace?

Swamiji: Because war is a time when everybody is in a different mood, on a different level of consciousness. Ordinarily, one wouldn't like to die, but in the war-spirit, one doesn't care for one's life.

Anjli: You mean it is like having declared a state of emergency when temporarily different rules and regulations come into operation. So the means are not to be considered at that time?

Swamiji: At that time, no.

Anjli: I suppose you mean that moral sensitivity at such a time reaches a low ebb. With this statement of yours, might one infer that nuclear warfare is justified, that germ warfare is justified because the means are not to be considered in war?

Swamiji: They are justified, because it is war.

Anjli: But what will happen to the world?

Swamiji: The world will suffer. But to the warrior at that moment all weapons are justified. Poor world will have to go through the suffering. Is it not suffering because of so many actions of ours? That is the outcome of war.

Anjli: Then all responsible decisions should be made prior to the war? But how in the Mahābhārata, which is such a special moral epic....

Swamiji: No, it is not. It is an epic, that's all. It is only giving an honest slice of life *as it is.* It is not life idealized. It is life *as it is:* a cross section of life brought to the vivid recognition of the average person, because the average person does not have a total vision of the vulgar things around. In the midst of it all is shown one vibrant character, always in equipoise, whether in the warfront, while telling a lie, while hugging his wife, or while kicking somebody, as always balanced! That fellow alone has the butter, the final goal in hand!!

Bhiṣma's Justification

Anjli: Should not the great Bhiṣma, prior to the call for war, and after negotiations broke down, have made it clear to the Kauravas that he would not take part in the war? It is said that he had partaken of their salt, but actually the Kauravas were beholden to him for the kingdom as well as for the regency. And if he could not convince them to desist from fighting, should he have joined them?

Swamiji: It is not because of this superficial reason that Bhiṣma joined the Kauravas. Bhiṣma himself gave the reason in an autobiographical backflash from the bed of arrows. The war was over, he was dying. But

he did not die because he had been given a boon by his father that
he could choose the time of his death. So he ordered Arjuna to make
a bed of arrows for him. But Bhisma didn't die because he had not
yet willed himself to die. It was at this time that Krishna told Yudhisthira
not to waste time, but to ask his uncle why he joined the Kauravas—
the same question.

Anjli: You mean Krishna and I asked the same question?

Swamiji: Yes, the same! Yudhisthira should go and ask Bhisma because
he was the only one who could answer this question. For all times it
would remain a question—why should such a *dharmanista purusa*
(righteous and noble person) join these tyrranical and unethical
people? Why should Bhisma have fought against Krishna especially
when he was the only man who knew at that time that Krishna was
divine. So Yudhisthira approached Bhisma and asked him that
question. Suddenly Bhisma turned to his right and said, "O Bhagavan!"
An ordinary commentary explains it as "Ah!" depicting pain, and it
shows Bhisma as answering the question. It is only Madhusudhana
Sarasvathi who says in his commentary that even while dying, the
brilliant master was sensible enough to judge that this question could
not have arisen from his nephew. He knew it must have been put to
him by Krishna. So after uttering "O Bhagavan! O Krishna," Bhisma
goes on with a backflash. He explains how from early childhood he
had to take a vow and renounce his aspirations for the kingdom to
facilitate his father's marriage to a young fisherwoman. After that
event Bhisma wanted to go away. But the father said that how could
he be sure he would get another child? And if the child happened to
be a female, Bhisma could not go away because a woman could not
rule. So Bhisma had to wait until the succession to the throne was
ensured. Then came the children. Their mother died in delivery.
The two little children and the father were seriously ill. So Bhisma
could not leave. He waited; the father never recovered and died. So
Bhisma had to become a protector, a regent in the name of his two
brothers. The two boys grew up, but they were so weak that they
required continual protection from Bhisma. Then he thought he
could leave when they begot children. But Bhisma's two brothers
died soon after. Their children were Dhrtharastra and Pandu. When
the elder one came of age, being blind he could not rule the kingdom. So Bhisma had to wait until the younger one grew up. And
again he was packing when the younger boy went to the forest for
hunting and killed a *brahmin* by mistake and then came back to his
grand uncle and said "I am going for *tapas*" (penance). Bhisma could

not stop him. So he continued to look after the kingdom. The two princes had no children. The blind man was not well. So Krishna advised them to organize a ritual as a result of which one got a hundred children and the other got five children. The blind man could not rule and the other brother had gone to the jungle for *tapas*. The hundred and five children were all with Bhisma, and he had to look after them. Then only he understood: "Five times I had packed in order to see you in the Himalayas. I took a lifetime vow of celibacy I had nothing to do with the kingdom, but five times something or the other happened. O Lord! I understood that you wanted me to be on their side, and to stay here. Knowing full well that I am such a devotee of yours, you wanted me here. All right, I also decided that I would be with them, whatever may happen, through thick and thin. War started; you promised that you would not lift a weapon, and I vowed publicly that I will make you take up a weapon. Now it is a war, O Lord! How kind you are; In order to make my vow truthful, you ultimately took a weapon and with the *Chakra* (discus) killed me. What more do I want?"

Anjli: Krishna killed Bhisma?

Swamiji: *Chakra* refers to *Sudarsan Chakra*. The *Chakra* of the Lord is called *Sudarsan* - the Great Vision. That is what Bhisma saw and exclaimed, "Now I don't mind. I have been rewarded completely. I am not dying yet because the Uttarayana* has not come. Therefore I am just waiting for another three more days. When Uttarayana starts, then if you will me to die, let me die."

Now it is by that portion of the Mahabharata that Bhisma's entire justification comes up. Superficially looking, one does talk about the "salt" aspect. It is not salt, as you said, no. It is not their salt, rather these people are eating his salt.

Anjli: But why did he side with the wicked hundred? He was equally beholden to stay with the five brothers. I mean, all along he had brought them up too.

Swamiji: He was in the palace. He was not anywhere else. The palace came under the hundred. So he remained in the palace because he knew that to get away from there was against the Lord's wish. "Five times I tried, five times some obstacle came. Therefore the Lord's wish is different." That is how he viewed it.

Anjli: Here is an example of how only the individual himself can determine his own *dharma*.

---

* northern path traced by the sun

Vegetarianism

Anjli: Now I would like to ask you some questions on food. What kind
of food do you recommend?

Swamiji: What you eat is your concern, not mine.

Anjli : Why is vegetarian food considered better in India?

Swamiji: Eat we must. What we like to eat depends upon one's taste.
There are only four things available—stones, plants, animals, and
humans. Unfortunately we cannot eat stones because our system is
not geared to digest and assimilate them directly. Human beings we
sometimes destroy in our cruelty, but we are not in the habit of eating
them like cutlets or side plates since our progressive culture does not
allow it. The only thing left to choose from is either the vegetable or
the animal kingdom. No doubt, since prehistoric times animals have
been eaten, but we find that the very first progenitor of humanity,
Adam himself, was eating only vegetables. It is only his second son
who started this easy method of obtaining food because agriculture
seemed to be too difficult for him as it required a continuous process
of putting forward effort in order to produce. Whereas sitting
behind a stone, waiting for innocent animals to come along, and
destroying and eating them seemed to be the easiest way!

Anjli : Maybe Adam was having the meat too!

Swamiji: It does not look to be so from the material available. I was not
there with Adam. I never had any dinner invitation from him!

Anjli: Perhaps you could have been the first person invited to taste the
apple!!
What about in the Vedic period? Why is sacrificing animals allowed
in the Scriptures, especially for rituals? If it is prohibited in daily life,
why do it at a time which was considered sacred?

Swamiji: In the Vedic period, animal worship and animal sacrifice were
conducted. There is evidence to prove that upto the Bhagavatam
time, we as Indians were nonvegetarians. It is only later on that the
idea of vegetarianism developed into a system.

Anjli: Perhaps it was due to geological events that increased the heat in
India and because meat decays faster that vegetarianism crept in.

Swamiji: We find that vegetables do not decay so fast, say upto forty
eight hours, they look fresh. But in forty eight hours, meat looks very
dirty, unless it is refrigerated. The deterioration of meat is faster.
Furthermore within the human body, during the process of digestion,
food remains in the canal for about forty eight hours. Meat takes a

very long time to digest. Fruit and vegetables get digested faster. Whatever stays longer in the intestines starts decaying and rotting with the heat of the body system, and a lot of toxins are created. Also, you must have noticed that generally man eats only those animals that don't eat other animals. It is very difficult for man to digest and assimilate carniverous animals. They must be toxic to his system. That means a certain amount of toxity is present in the first round, because twice removed the meat becomes impossible to eat!

Anjli: That means nonvegetarians are safe from cannibals!

Swamji: Ha! Ha!

Anjli: Seriously, this is as far as the body goes, and what one eats is between the doctor and the person who wants to remain healthy. But in what way does vegetarian food help a person's mind? Did people discover that it affects the mental temperament?

Swamiji: The food that we take in and the thoughts and actions that spring forth from us have a distinct relationship. Garbage in, garbage out, is the great saying of the computer language, and it seems to be true that if you put garbage within your system, in the long run the texture of your thoughts and actions have a tendency to become more unreconciling, extremely selfish, less concerned for others, lusty, and therefore dangerous to the social order.

Now if you use a common social argument and say that if we don't eat animals, they will multiply to such an extent that they will have to be curtailed by man eating them, I ask you to apply this argument to the human level also and then you will understand the absurdity of it. Let all the people who are sick be killed by you and eaten. Young ones who have not yet started life you kill and eat thereby the food problem will be solved, population problem will also be solved in one and the same stroke. This is not fair. Nature has various other methods of keeping the balance. Man need not struggle with his tiny little mouth to keep nature in balance. Toxins in the system bring about a lot of mental disturbances. The same principle applies to drinks. Since our culture is essentially geared for the life of meditation, the mind that is constantly agitated and wandering finds it difficult to plunge into meditation. To such an individual, the toxin is a danger to reach his goal. Probably this must have been the reason why the *rishis* in the jungles ate only fruits, roots, leaves, and water. Those who take nonvegetarian food, because of the toxins, are very uncontrolled. Watch a nonvegetarian and a vegetarian animal. All herbaceous animals are available for eating; the non-vegetarian or carniverous animals are never eaten even by a professional nonvegetarian! Because carniverous animals have got so much toxin in them that it means almost death if not sickness or a serious illness.

Anjli: Some Chinese eat it and our tribal people also.

Swamiji: They somehow or the other kill it and tie it down and plaster it with some herbs. Then a kind of water drips out of the meat, maybe carrying some toxins out.

Anjli: Probably like our *karela,* the bitter gourd vegetable.

Swamiji: You boil it and pour it away, boil it and pour it away so that the bitterness is reduced, probably something like that, and then you eat it.

A carniverous animal is never tamed. Take a tiger or lion. In the circus people do it and if the lion gets angry and you happen to give
· him a chance the lion tamer becomes his lunch! It is evident that the mind becomes soft and receptive and available for training only when it is mellow and it had been found that vegetarian food makes the mind more mellow, more plastic and the personality is gentle rather than vicious.

Anjli: But doesn't the tiger have a better personality than a donkey?

Swamiji: Yes! Do you want a personality or a character? What is that you want? We are talking of culture and not beauty.

Anjli: How come westerners who are mostly nonvegetarian are healtheir than us vegetarians?

Swamiji: To say that vegetarians are unhealthy is also not very true because vegetarians like the camel have stamina and elephant have sheer size and strength and horses are sturdy and beautiful. So it is not very right to say this and these are silly arguments that were brought in at a time when everybody thought that eating dead bodies is the best way of living. Nowadays the whole opinion has changed, but I will come to that. Also the world has recognized the economics of it recently. They have made statistics that were published all over; I think UNO did it, about the amount of land necessary for cattle to feed. That it is uneconomical to leave so much land fallow for cattle to feed on and also much of the grains are given as fodder to animals to fatten on so that the meat may be good. This land, if used for growing more food, can be used to feed more people in the world and the starvation level can be wiped out completely. It is not correct to say that in order to have stamina a lot of meat is necessary. In fact, the latest theory is that this animal protein is very difficult to be digested and assimilated and that vegetable proteins are more easily absorbed in the system.

The climatic condition in the west forced them to eat meat because they could not have vegetarian food all the year round. For three or four months only could they plough the land, the rest of the time it is all snow. As you come more and more towards the tropical climate, there is more greenery, more vegetables are available.

Anjli: Does vegetarian food help meditation?

Swamiji: Even great thinkers and meditators like Jesus took only bread and water while in the desert, similarly our sages and saints. Even kings and others while living in the palace might have been taking meat but when they went for *tapas* or austerities and meditation into the forests they switched on to lighter food, that is, vegetarian food, especially, for our climate. The reason why it became over-emphasized in the Mahābhārata time was, I think, because by then India's climatic condition changed. Earlier the snow line was so near the Ganga at Haridwar or at Gandanani or even at Gangotri. Then it began to recede further with the result that the climatic condition also changed. The Thar dessert asserted itself because the snow line receded or the snow line receded because of the dessert's onslaught. Population increased, deforestation took place. So many reasons were there. Afforestation had been ignored therefore climatic conditions changed. Therefore, I think that it was in the time of the Bhagawatam that they advertised dairy farming and vegetarianism the maximum. In India whenever a health order or sanitary rule was to be popularized or promulgated they always did it riding on religious concepts.

Anjli: So it was Vyāsa who started it?

Swamiji: It is in the Mahābhārata that we find this emphasized more and more and the pajan of this philosophy is Krishna and especially the emphasis on dairy farms. So Govardhanoddhārak is the name. *Go* - cows, *vardhan* - development of cattle, *uddhārak* - one who gives a fillip to cattle breeding or maintaining a better cadre.

Anjli: It is said that Aryans introduced the cow population in India. Prior to that there were only buffaloes just as in Africa and Asia upto Japan as India falls into the same geographic belt as them. It was to preserve this newly introduced species that it was recommended by the priest class that to eat beef is irreligious?

Swamiji: Maybe.

Anjli: If as you say vegetarian food tames the mind and the character of a person becomes less viscious, how come it had the opposite effect on Hitler? He was a vegetarian.

Swamiji: Your two or three questions are aimed at asking whether vegetarian food will change the character of an individual. No. It is the other way round. The character of the individual personality determines the type of food that he will find a taste for. The eighteenth chapter of the Bhagavad Gītā indicates definitely what kind of food the individual will find tasty who is under the awe of *sattva*, *rajas*, or *tamas*. So it is not that Hitler was a vegetarian so how come he killed so many million people.

Anjli: All right. Let's put it this way. How come his kind of character found vegetarian food tasty!

Swamiji: What I meant was that whatever food you are eating it is the mood of the mind that determines the choice and from his standpoint and level he did not feel anything wrong. He was probably calculating that during the First World War how many people died and how many of his Germans died. He wanted to reorganize his country. How was he going to reorganize his country? These are the community of people standing against the progress— that was his way of thinking. —See! his anger turned that way, and a German is such that whatever he does he does it thoroughly. And he did it thoroughly! Now don't misunderstand, I am not supporting his theory. But his intentions from where he was looking at the problem were at the level of *rajoguna** at its highest pitch wherein he had sunk into the lowest depth of maybe gone crazy. Once you get angry you can go crazy. And poor fellow he happened to be at the top of things. So then, there is no end.

Anjli: His moral sensitivity was low—what we talked about earlier. You were saying that the character of an individual personality finds a liking for a particular type of food. Does this liking indicate anything subjective?

Swamiji: Vegetarian food by itself cannot make you a noble person. When your mind is bending toards *rājasic* and *tāmasic* traits, these tastes will come in your mind which will be a kind of panel dashboard indicator indicating the condition of the machine inside. A red light comes which indicates that the dynamo is not charging, or whatever it is. Similarly, while sitting, I suddenly feel the desire to go out and eat *golgappas*** because it is a Sunday and I have nothing else to do.... but such a thought will not come on an active Monday morning while going to the office. I am just giving an example. So thereby I don't say that really pure vegetarians from birth onward don't do anything violent.

Many are in jails for even murder. So it is not eating the food that

---

* Feverish activity
** Spicy Indian delicacy

determines your character or your tendencies but the mental tendencies that give a taste, a special taste in your mind, a taste in you for such food. So whenever we find that the mind is tending towards *rājasic* or *tāmasic* food and drink as enumerated in eighteenth chapter of Bhagavad Gītā, immediately remember to tune up the mind's attention to the higher from the lower as this is an indicator.

Anjli: You would not recommend that a person should turn vegetarian unless he has an inner inclination?

Swamiji: No. I don't want him to become a vegetarian forcefully. But very many people become vegetarians because it happens to be the trend. Just as one tries drugs because it happens to be the trend. Similarly one can introduce vegetarianism as a positive trend among people. For instance, if a person gets chronic headaches, one can recommend vegetarian food for a period of two months. The headache may or may not go but the person feels happy with that food. Having tried it he doesn't find it so bad. One can recommend but not force anyone or insist upon it. The individual must himself decide after trying it "Am I unhappy?". If not, try it once or twice a week and then slowly build it up. The sensitivity of the mind also builds up and he feels a cultural call that to satisfy one and a half inches of his tongue he has taken the life of a conscious being.

Anjli: Plants also have life.

Swamiji: But animal life is more evolved, so spare them.

Anjli: But plants have feelings too. They show reactions when you experiment on them.

Swamiji: Yes. But they are as if in a chloroform condition just as when you operate on a human being he feels the pain without anesthesia, but under anesthesia or chloroform he does not feel the pain, though he has life. So we take for our food from the plant kingdom giving minimum sorrow to life all around. Even that is a harm. But what do do? There is no other option; stones you can't eat, dead bodies you can't, then only plants are there. So then we generally pray before eating food, "O Lord. I am becoming indebted again to these in front of me. They have sacrificed so that my life may be protected and may their sacrifice be rewarding." Just as in the army so many people die for the country so that others may live in improved conditions later. This becomes the government's responsibility. Similarly, it is our responsibility that the food that has been destroyed for our growth may be justified when we progress to become noble human beings. Just as, if after the war, conditions are worse, then it is a great loss. That is the idea.

Anjli: This should make one careful not to waste food.
Growing children require a lot of protein. Meat etc. have all the eight
superior quality amino acids that go into making protein, whereas
no one vegetarian food item has them. You generally have to com-
bine several vegetable protein foods in order for it to be equivalent
to the quality of protein in nonvegetarian food.

Swamiji: Even the mother's milk you don't give and then you start
giving chemicals. That is how you start the life of children. A mother's
milk is just sufficient for them in the beginning—later on you add the
other milk, curd, pulses and you build up. It is quite a healthy diet,
a vegetarian diet, a I told you earlier.....

Anjli: Yes, I remember. The stamina of the camel, strength of the
elephant, and beauty of the horse come from vegetarian food. You
did not mention that gorillas are the strongest and most long lived of
all the homosapiens. They are not only vegetarians but are only
fruitarians! Swamiji, you take insulin for your diabetes and it is made
from animal substance?

Swamiji: Food is medicine. Medicine is not food. For medicinal purposes you are allowed to take. Even in Ayurveda* itself there are
preparations which are nonvegetarian that are considered. For
tuberculosis and other diseases some nonvegetarian preparations
are recommended. So that is a medicine. So the Swami can get
injection of the pig's pancreas! Pancreas from the pig is taken, that
is insulin.

Anjli: So you have no choice.

Swamiji: No choice! Because artificially it cannot be made.

Anjli: Some of the world's great scientists have been nonvegetarians.

Swamiji: Yes. And among the greatest thinkers and scientists also they
have discovered for themselves, unfortunately much too late in life,
that vegetarian food is better, that the quality of thinking is better.
That is why Einstein later on, become a pure vegetarian. Bernard
Shaw— a pure vegetarian. We don't say nonvegetarian will make you
dull but it would have been....

Anjli: What I mean is that the west has produced all these people
whereas we vegetarians have not produced any scientists as such.

Swamiji: A lot of difference. Their research is on the grosser side, the
outer world. Here the development is on the subtler side, the within.
Our research has been subjective. For knowing the subtle, the mind
has to be that much more precisely perfect.

---

* ancient Indian medicinal system.

Cessation of External Conflicts

Meera: Can you envisage some time in the future when men will naturally lead a moral life, or do you think that the conflict and tension between good and evil will remain always?

Swamiji: Always. That is the nature of the world. This will always be there. If it is not there then they will be in heaven. It will be there. Living in contrarities is universal. Don't come under it. That is moral living. Not that immoral thoughts will not come. But the moral man is one who does not allow such things to express through him. Then in the long run it dies out. Then you become really liberated.

Care of the physical body

Meera: Is surrender to the needs of the physical body *per se* sinful?

Swamiji: Don't be indifferent to the sense objects says the Upaniṣad. The physical body is to be looked after because it is the instrument for *mokṣa* (liberation). The body, therefore, is a means for *mokṣa*. A seeker, in the beginning, must look after the body very well. And when you live the *dharma* of your station in life in the desireless attitude, the mind gets chastened.....

Intense Love

Anjli: Does love for a human being, if very intense, help one to the path of spirituality?

Swamiji: Yes, it does.

Anjli: How is that? Even when there is a physical elemen· in it which may draw one away from the finer and spiritual aspect?

Swamiji: Then it is not love, it is lust.

Anjli: But you once said that love like Laila-Majnu's....

Swamiji: Love! Love in the sense that I am enchanted by some noble quality of another individual. Not merely because it's one hundred and forty pounds of flesh, tha·'s very superficial. What I said was love. Love is only generated because of my admiration of some noble quality in the other individual. It is purely because of his knowledge, his way of living, his way of conducting society that we admire him. So love for a person like Rāmakrishna Paramhansa, Vivekananda, I

don't say that they may not have imperfections — but those we
overlook. It is not for that. Krishna—I mean devotion to Krishna—
another fellow might emphasize all the weaknesses in Krishna but is
the devotee looking at the weaknesses or the glory or the beauty? So
true love, when generated, is always due to the noble qualities in a
person.

Anjli: Does it become a higher love depending upon the qualities of the
person we love?

Swamiji: The emotion is the same in both the higher and the lower
kinds of love. When we direct our love towards a higher, a more
inspiring ideal, our minds expand, our faculties broaden, our vision
deepens and our efficiencies multiply. When the same emotion of
love goes towards external objects of pleasure, things or beings, it
slowly shells us into a life of tensions and anxieties, into a prison of
sorrows and excitements, pangs and sobs. It is then that we really
"fall" in love!

Anjli: How can we know that our love is noble?

Swamiji: We "rise" in love when love is true and dynamic and there is a
great joy felt in giving love rather than meekly hoping to receive.
Love is its own reward. Such a person is not a beggar at love's
temple-gate. Very few realize this; no one dares to live it in life. To
give love is true freedom, to demand love is pure slavery.

Anjli: What would you say is the highest moral advice?

Swamiji: Love is the highest moral truth and hence "love thyself" is the
greatest moral injunction if the seeker does not misunderstand the
advice. It does not mean loving the body or obeying the mind meekly.
The mind and intellect are gross matter envelopments that have
come to seemingly limit the illimitable Supreme Consciousness
which is the real Self in all of us. When the seeker's mind melts
in the warmth of his single pointed love for God, the Self in us, the
sublime fusion of the finite with the Infinite takes place.

A Summing Up

Anjli: In summing up certain ethical problems that come up in the
context of particular social situations, Swamiji, you have explained
that in general no moral situation is dogmatic. Its evaluation often
depends upon factors outside the obvious ones whether in the case
of enthanasia, abortion, political and economic pressures, the *sati*
practice, vegetarianism or in the moral decisions of great men

during their fight between good and evil. It is important to analyze these decisions as they tend to have historical repercussions. Such decisions ought to be based on the higher values of life and for the welfare of society in general thereby ennobling man and helping him towards the goal of self-realization.

This becomes necessary because a person's choice of action or his field of functioning, including the food he eats, the kind of person he loves, reflect the values that he upholds in life. If his values are higher, his actions are better.

We need to train ourselves to be socially sensitive, but this is best achieved by dedicating our activities to a higher goal. A superficial facelifting of society by social workers without trying to improve themselves does not achieve lasting results.

Love of God is the highest moral truth which expresses in the world as giving rather than receiving, in an irresistable dash into the hearts of all, culminating in the sublime fusion of the finite with the Infinite.

Swamiji, in case there are further questions arising from the answers you have so patiently and obligingly given, I hope it will be in order to join you in another journey, preferably one which takes us even further beyond!